Diary of a young Jewish girl

WORLD WAR II
HUNGARY 1941-1946

Madelaine D. Lang

Self published by Madelaine D. Lang with Createspace
2012

ISBN-10: 1475206623
ISBN 13: 978-1475206623

United States of America
Registration Number
TXu 1-753-731
May 3, 2011

In the memory of my Father, who died in 1944.
And to the memory of 600,000 Hungarian Jews
who perished in the Holocaust

ACKNOWLEDGEMENTS

I want to thank my three sons, who first encouraged me to translate my old diary from Hungarian to English, and who then helped me and guided me to create a book for all to read the historic background of my young life during the war.

I also thank my husband for his enthusiasm in my endeavor to tell my story to the public, and for all to learn how I found a way to survive the persecution of the Jews in Hungary.

Finally I would also like to thank all of my dear friends and family members who read the early drafts and provided helpful comments and feedback to me.

TABLE OF CONTENTS

INTRODUCTION

L ooking for something among some old papers, I surprisingly found my diary that I had written seventy years ago during my school years and during the Second World War. Upon the request of my three sons, I have now translated it from Hungarian to English. I need to explain a bit about my life, so one can better understand my living circumstances before the war. Before I start on my diary I want to paint a picture of our everyday life in Miskolc, where I was born. At that time Miskolc was the second largest city in Hungary and a lively commercial hub surrounded by the Bukk Mountains on one side and Tapolca, a beautiful thermal resort, on the other side with a few rivers and creeks bordering and crisscrossing the town.

First I want to start talking about my father, whom I loved dearly and whom I lost during the deportation of the Jews in Budapest. I knew very little about his childhood. I only knew that he went to a commercial business school in Miskolc and that his first job was in a candy factory. From the candy factory job, he joined the military. When World War I started in 1914, he was twenty-four years old and was sent to the Russian front. Not too long after he arrived at the front, he was taken prisoner and sent to Siberia along with his peers.

He was kept for four years until the war ended in 1918. Many times he told me about his experiences as a young man away from his home and family, including time in the camp. He told me about eggs being sold in large sacks like walnuts, and the eggs

SIBERIA.
MY FATHER IN KRASNOYARSK, 1916.

were completely frozen. Another story focused on his roommate in the camp who received a package from home with some food and only one boot. His roommate was so furious that the other boot must have been stolen that he threw it out over the prison camp fence. The next month he received another package from home that had the other boot!

When the war ended the Allies dissolved the Austro-Hungarian Empire. The Kingdom of Hungary became Truncated Hungary after the Treaty of Trianon in 1920. The Allies gave the northern part of Hungary to Czechoslovakia, although it changed hands again in 1938 - 1940 and was given to Slovakia because most of Slovakia had a Hungarian population. I mention this fact because throughout my diary you can read about how this back-and-forth change affected our lives.

By the time my father returned home he was twenty-eight years old. His older brother was married and had two children, a boy, Laci and a girl, Manci. Laci was at law school, and Manci was married to an attorney and had a beautiful

DRUCKER FAMILY. ALL TOGETHER WITH MY FATHER, MOTHER AND I.

little boy, Adam. They all lived together on my grandparent's large property where there was a home for the old couple, another apartment for the older son and his family and a large wholesale bakery, supplying bread, rolls, and croissants to the retail stores throughout the city. I can still smell the fresh baked goods as I think about it. Laci's father was a salesman who sold flour from the mills to the merchants, while my father obtained a position in the Electrical Trust Company as a bookkeeper. He married my mother who was from Kassa, which then was a part of Hungary. Kassa had a fine Jewish center of educated and well-to-do families. Through the years my father worked his way up from a bookkeeper to the director of the company. He held that position while I was growing up. The Trust Company was the city's most important employer.

My grandfather died when I was still a little girl; I only remember him praying on Saturday nights with a braided candle (like my hair) wearing a nice velvet embroidered hat. After his death the bakery did not fare as well. My grandmother used to donate food and money to the poor Jews who came every Saturday to the bakery.(It was a custom to help the needy and the less fortunate.) My father gave my grandmother money so she could continue her charity. Every Saturday morning my father took me to see grandmother, but my mother would not come, she kept busy with other chores.

During the High Holidays half of the family belonged to the large synagogue on Paloczy Street, which later was bombed and completely destroyed. My parents belonged to the newer temple on Kazinczy Street, which was a Reform temple. When this new temple was built they installed an organ, which is when the congregation split. I remember we, the youngsters, went to visit both parents and grandparents from one temple to the other. (Women sat upstairs on the balcony) I was so happy when I turned thirteen because I could then fast on Yom Kippur and from then on I fasted every year on that Holy Day. During prayers I went out to the courtyard with my friends and waited until the ceremony was over and we could all go home. Father always had a chocolate with cherry liqueur in it to eat while he walked the long way home after fasting the whole day. At school, which was called a gimnazium, a private protestant school (Miskolci Reformatus Leany Gimnazium), we studied Hebrew reading and writing during religious classes, but I unfortunately was not very good at it. I did not understand what I read, unlike the other living languages, French and German. I simply accepted Hebrew as the language we prayed in the temple .

As a little girl and daughter of our city's leading citizen, I received most people's attention but not because of me. I received the attention because of my father, who was well liked and well respected. Being the only child, even as a girl, my father took me with him to football (what Americans call soccer) games. The Attila team of Miskolc had a very important place in the national championship, and he taught me the rules of the game, so I could know what I was watching and enjoy it with him. I also went with him to the neighboring villages where the company had its turbines built in the water, which used the flow of the river to generate electricity. The head of the plant was a nice man who lived in a wonderful house in the village with his family. They were extremely friendly with me. I enjoyed these excursions away from the hustle and bustle of the city where we lived and where I went to school. My father also took me to Budapest. He bought me a camera, a Voigtlander, and I proudly took my first photos of the city's famous statues, which I then showed my girlfriends. None of them had visited the capital at that age.

My mother was born in a city which changed hands many times between Slovakia and Hungary. (The Hungarian name was Nagymihaly and the Slovakian name was Michalovce). My grandfather had an agricultural produce business. My mother, who was the youngest, had three sisters and one brother. She went to school in Kassa/Kosice where she lived with her oldest sister, Szeren, who was already married. When she was 23 years old, she married to my father, who was from Miskolc in Hungary. His surname was Drucker, but he changed it to a more Hungarian sounding name Denes.

ZOLTAN AND KORNELIA.
Zoltan and Kornelia. My parent's wedding picture 1923.

When I was growing up, my mother dressed me well. She had good taste and was very particular in getting my clothes. When I was younger, not yet ten years old, a seamstress came to our house. My mother gave the seamstress her own dresses, which she had tired of wearing, to alter for me. Years later she bought nice fabrics, and the seamstress cut them for my clothes. I don't remember ever going to the store and buying something ready-made. Mother bought her dresses in the best fashion stores in Budapest. I actually took all these things for granted. We did not discuss money at home. Whenever I asked to buy something, my mother's decision to buy it was based not on whether we could afford it but rather on whether I needed it or not. I was not spoiled and was taught to use money smartly and sparingly. In the last year of elementary school I was cast in a play. I wore a beautiful pink taffeta dress with a big bow in my hair, and my mother took me to a portrait painter in that dress. She read *Huckleberry Finn* to me (in Hungarian) so I would sit

MY GRANDMOTHER.
My grandmother visiting Miskolc, wearing shawl, 1940

still while the painter painted my portrait. The painting is still decorating my son's living room wall.

We owned a nice house with a small garden and a one-room house (for the caretaker) that wasn't far from the city's center We had a live-in Austrian governess, and I spoke only German until I entered elementary school. I liked her a lot, and she could knit beautiful little dresses, scarves, and hats for my doll. She played with me and took me for walks and later to school and on visits to homes of nearby kids. During this time, I learned to speak Hungarian.

My grandmother on my mother's side spoke only German.

Even though I could converse with her, I never felt really close to her. When she came to visit from Kassa, there was excitement in our home. I went with my mother to the market to buy fresh fruits and vegetables. Miskolc had a large outdoor market where the peasants sold everything from chickens and geese to eggs, fresh butter and cheeses. The produce was brought in from the villages by the cartload. Meanwhile at home, the maid cleaned the rooms and the kitchen in preparation of my grandmother's arrival. My grandmother ate only kosher, and my mother made sure that she would eat in our home. Of course, I was curious to see how they cooked and baked. I licked the sweets when they didn't see me until they threw me out of the kitchen.

Grandma was from Graz, Austria, and got married to my grandfather in Nagymihaly, which was then Hungary. He owned a good business in agricultural produce. When he died, she moved to Kassa, where her two daughters and son lived with their families. They were all within walking distance from each other, and every day she visited one or the other on her daily walk. My grandfather died when I was very young, and I really do not remember him.

MAGDA AT SPA.
Called "strand" in Miskolc.

Early one morning I woke up to a great commotion and noticed a strong smell of smoke in the house. I discovered that we had a fire in our living room, which luckily was quickly extinguished. Later mother told me that the maid came in early, while we were all sleeping, to clean and dust the furniture, sofa, armchairs, and my father's desk. A white marble stand with a vase on it and an electric cigarette lighter was also in the room. As the maid was dusting, the lighter fell. The maid left the room and did not hear the lighter fall. It unfortunately and curiously fell on its knob, which ignited the lighter and started the fire. The armchairs covered with fine velour first sparked into flames. Fortunately, even in those days, father had everything insured, so mother replaced it with even better quality and more elegant furniture.

During the summers I spent a lot of time with the young boys and girls my age at the spa, which belonged to the Trust company, and of course, was free of charge for us. The spa had two swimming pools where I learned to swim when I was ten years old, tennis courts where my parents played (I was not good at tennis), and a small restaurant. All in all, it was the best resort without having to travel far.

Even the tram to the spa was free for me. I remember that at home we did not have electric meters, because the electricity was free too. In spite of that my father taught me how to save electricity. I had to shut off everything the minute it was no longer in use. For good measure, my father received honorary tickets to the theater for seats in the second row, (the first was too close to the stage), and he took me sometimes to a play when the famous actors and actresses came down from Budapest.

By the time I was ready to start the gimnazium, (like a lycee) at the age of ten, my mother found a beautiful home in the city's center, in a residential street close to everything. It was walking distance to the school, shops, theater, movie house, and the Small-Holder Club, where my parents played cards and met all their friends. The home was a two story building; we owned the entire ground floor with the other owner living on the upper floor. This house also had a small garden, just enough to plant a few flowers, and a terrace, where we enjoyed

MAGDA WITH PARENTS.
MAGDA IN SCHOOL UNIFORM.

sitting in the sun when the weather was nice. Making some friends who were in my class and also lived nearby was easy. We were able to drop in anytime to see one another. We used no phones to communicate; phones existed for the adults and for emergencies. On the other hand the radio occupied an important part in our lives. We listened to good music and the news.

In the gimnazium, from ages ten to eighteen, I continued in the same class with the same pupils until we graduated and received our diploma.

The professors, men and women, also stayed the same and each taught a different subject. They were strict, demanding respect and expecting everyone to always be on their best behavior. The government mandated a standard curriculum in every school in every town, so if I would have to move with my parents anywhere in the country, I could continue my studies without difficulty. The compulsory subjects were German and French from the first grade and Latin from the third to the eighth year. We had a large gym, a room for physics and biology, and a separate building where we studied religion. The Protestant church privately owned the school, but everybody was taught their own religion, so the Catholics had their classes, the Jews theirs, and so on. I look back on this regimen, and I think it was very well organized. We also had a choir, though I was never good at singing.

The building upstairs housed a dormitory for students who were from out of town, and I befriended many of them. I remember well that during lunch time I would bring from home sandwiches with salami or cheese on a roll, and I exchanged them for bread with prune butter, which I loved. The school yard also had a place where we could buy some lunch. The janitor had a small booth and for a few *filler* (pennies of the local currency), he sold a cold sandwich, some cookies, or an apple, but no cooked meals. I enjoyed school. I was a good student and studying was easy. I paid attention to the teachers and could remember the subjects without having to study them at home, all except mathematics, which was my weakness. To keep up my good marks, I often went to my friend Z. Zsuzsi, who lived on the same street. She not only was the best in class she also was the best in the whole school. I did my homework with her.

Languages were my strongest subject. The principal, who taught literature, always read my written homework to the class as an example for the others. I remember once we had to write an essay on biology during class. I had no idea what it was about but succeeded to make the subject so interesting (without any facts) that again the teacher praised my work. However my mother was very strict with me regarding school. Not only did the professors pressure us to attain good marks, but my mother was even more demanding. She signed me up for private lessons, which I attended after school. I started to learn English and French, because what we learned in school was really not enough to master the language. I also studied piano when a piano teacher came to the house twice a week. As if that was not enough, I also went to a private class for Swedish exercises to keep in shape. When I practiced the piano, my mother sat next to me and she would get so upset if I hit the wrong note by mistake, that she made my life miserable. I enjoyed the music only when I played alone and no one was home. In the evenings I still had my homework to do.

I did not have much time for entertainment. Of course, TV did not exist in those days. In my spare time I met with the girls and together we strolled down Main Street where we met the boys, or we went to the public park when the weather was nice. Every summer an Italian opened an ice-cream store, and we all went, four or five of us, to spend our pocket money. We also enjoyed going to the movies. The cinema usually showed American films which we found so different from our way of life. These films gave us lots to talk about. We knew all the famous actors and actresses, and a few girls could even imitate them.

Books were another important part of my life growing up. I could read foreign books for hours, which were all translated into Hungarian, and which later I could also read in their original language. I enjoyed the most when I was able to read the author's own words. I remember when *Gone with the Wind* arrived and we talked about Scarlet O'Hara and Rhett Butler.

We all fell in love with him. I also read every book by Stefan Zweig. What a writer!

When we finished the eighth year, we received written permission from the principal of the school to prepare for the diploma to graduate. Getting ready to graduate was very serious and very difficult. We all had to study hard to make sure we passed the written and oral exams. I used to get up at six in the morning and go to the cemetery, which was a short walk from home, to study undisturbed in the quiet park. I took my books with me to scan through the material that we had learned the past eight years, while sitting on some benches between the tombstones. Though I spoke perfect German, I was worried that I might make mistakes with the grammar, so I decided to brush up and take private lessons to give me the extra confidence during the final test. I actually did so well that the teacher wrote a remark on my paper. Not only did I translate it word by word, but I also recaptured the story's mood. My mother was finally satisfied. We had a beautiful ceremony with all the girls walking through the classroom around the benches where we had sat during the past eight years, holding hands and singing *Gaudeamus Igitur,* the song that so many students sang before us every year on this occasion.

In Miskolc our family has completely assimilated into the Hungarian lifestyle, culture, literature, food and clothing. I grew up as a Hungarian Jewish girl, and it did not make any difference in our lives that I went to a Protestant school. My class had ten Jewish girls, and somehow instinctively we shared a warmer, closer friendship, compared to the other non-Jewish students. But once Hitler's Nazi influence spread around us, we realized that we were a people persecuted and hated simply because we were born Jewish. Until 1942 we had equal rights and lived without any problems. In fact, we had contributed in every way to the life and culture of Miskolc. My parents were able to travel abroad without restrictions. When I was only fifteen, my father took me on a ship down the Danube River to the Black Sea and to Istanbul; it was a beautiful vacation.

I spent all my Christmas and summer vacations in Kassa with my mother's family, growing up with my cousins. Kassa was a more cultured, rich city with many Jewish merchant families; Miskolc was a commercial center with a nearby large ironworks factory. I enjoyed being in Kassa more, because in the summer my cousin Dudi was a member of a large circle of very bright youths and we often went swimming together in the pool or hiking in the nearby woods; we also had home parties and went to the movies (where we occupied a whole row) During the winter we ice-skated on the frozen pond. We drank hot wine to warm up and I really enjoyed being part of the group. I was happy that they took me with them even though I was younger. In the school these students all studied the Slovak language until the city changed hands when Hungary annexed Slovakia in 1938. After that, students had to learn Hungarian. Dudi had a very nice schoolmate, a Christian girl from a very rich family. One day she took me with her to their home to see the beautiful tall Christmas tree with all the decorations hanging on it. She told me about all the gifts she was getting. This was all new to me; none of my friends in Miskolc had anything like this.

In Kassa one of the boys already had a car, a Tatra convertible.

Tatra Auto, Dudi's friends in Kassa

We had lots of fun with it, at least eight of us packed into it. That car gave me the idea that when I will graduate from the gimnazium I should buy a car too. I had my eye on a beautiful small BMW for quite some time. I started to save my pocket money, but unfortunately by 1942 the government confiscated all private automobiles, so instead, my parents bought me a very nice daybed with my money that I had saved. When we later moved to Budapest my bed followed me like a faithful dog. Could I have slept on my automobile? PERHAPS IN MY DREAMS COULD I HAVE SLEPT IN MY AUTOMOBILE?

Mother always had live-in maids, and when she heard that a family had returned from Canada to a nearby village with two daughters, she contacted the family. She offered the younger one, Julie,

who already had finished high school in Canada, to live with us as a quasi-governess and to spend time with me and help me improve my English. The private English lessons I had taken up

Julie, my Canadian Governess.

to that point taught me only vocabulary and grammar. Julie was well compensated and I was very happy to have her. Of course at the same time, my mother learned to speak English too. What a blessing this proved to be later in my life.

By writing about my family's lives in such detail, I want to share the tremendous difference in my quality of life that followed from 1942 after my graduation.

My whole life was turned upside down with the Nazi era. Simply because my father was Jewish, he was forced to resign from his position as director of the company and was drafted and removed to a labor camp. We had to give up our home and move to Budapest into much more modest conditions. The pages that follow are my original diary that I wrote from the ages of seventeen to twenty-two. Here I describe my family's lives at the time of the onslaught of the Nazis in Hungary and how my life changed completely from a privileged young girl with a high sense of self-esteem to a young Jewish girl fighting for her life.

CHAPTER 1

It is 1940, Easter in Miskolc. I bought this notebook to start a diary; I have so much to say.

As I entered my room, someone jumped on my back and, when

DUDI. My cousin from Kassa.

I turned around, kissed me all over. It was Dudi, my cousin from Kassa.

She was a real surprise. She came down to Miskolc by car with Uncle Gyula and now mother wants to return with him to Kassa. We chattered to no end and asked each other about everything, but then I had to study English. I had to go for my lesson after lunch since this week we had no school. When I came back, I sat down to play the piano and then to French lessons. This of course I do every day, and I could not skip just because Dudi arrived.

In the evening my father suggested we go to a movie. Uncle Gyula had not picked up mother yet, so she will probably leave while we are away. We saw Queen Victoria a beautiful British film. Of course it was synchronized, as most foreign films are and the Hungarians were known to be very good at it. Watching the actors you would think they spoke Hungarian. Tonight I will sleep together with Dudi in the big bed, and we will put father on the couch.

Next morning Julie joined us in bed. When mother hired her to be our English teacher and she moved in with us, mother had arranged a daybed for her in the dining room, it was so big there was plenty space for her to be comfortable. Dudi was telling us stories about Kassa. The maid could hardly get us out from under the covers. Finally we all got ready and went for a walk. We met Bandi and stopped at the pastry shop. He ordered for all of us. He chose a lot of sweets and placed them on our table. I don't know if he wanted to show off in front of Dudi, but he behaved terribly. He then paid for all, which of course none of us permitted him to do, and finally we pushed one pengo in his hand. As we left the shop, he gave it to the first poor child we met on the street. I told him this cannot go on; a gentleman does not behave this way. But he did not listen to me—he is a big, unmanageable child, and I can make no excuse for him. Dudi said the same thing. A normal, smart adult does not behave this way. But he thinks he is right and will not listen to anyone. He lives in his own world, in his dreams. Since I see all his faults, why do I love him? Why don't I despise him, push him away. And why don't

I instead go with Gyuri? He is an angel compared to Bandi. He has a wonderful nature. He's sober, with sound judgment, and he does not have unattainable dreams. I enjoy meeting him on our outings to the Bukk Mountains on weekends. He is more mature than Bandi; of course, he is also three years older than me.

Julie was giving English lessons this morning to other students she had, so she was already up at eight. Dudi and I stayed in bed and were chatting when I saw some flowers being delivered. Yesterday we had stopped in front of a flower shop where they had live white rabbits in the window. "Oh, they are so cute! I would love to have one!" said Dudi. I told her right away to watch what she says. Bandi was with us and he heard it. And now they are here. She did not believe it until the maid brought them in to us. Three little white rabbits with red eyes sat on a red tulle bed chewing on carrots. They were so pretty. We did not know what to do first—it was such a pleasure, but at the same time an annoyance, that someone could be so foolish to surprise us this way. We racked our brains on how to avenge this so that he should have just as much trouble as we will have with these rabbits, but we could think of nothing.

Julie had not seen them yet. They each had a ribbon on their neck with our monograms.

As we went for a walk we met Bandi and thanked him for the gift. We also met Laci (my cousin), whom we walked home with, and Julie joined us, by now she had seen everything at home. We could hardly eat lunch; we kept running to the rabbits to play with them and to clean up the room after them. There was no end to taking care of them. We took apart the cage and put the flowers into water. In other words, we did not have a quiet moment.

In the afternoon we went to a movie and saw a Hungarian film,—not too famous. That evening we went for a walk again, and we bought perfume for Bandi. I wonder how he will react to that. He has to accept it. We were in the middle of dinner when Laci arrived; he planned to go with father to the Small-Holder's Club, where they mostly played cards, but of course he could not resist three girls. Father left and we turned on the radio. There was excellent jazz on the air, and we started to dance. Laci seemed to have a good time while he danced with each of us. We drank some liqueur and ate small, homemade cookies. Julie got tipsy—she was very cute. Laci went home, and we put everything back in order. We had an enjoyable evening.

LACI DRUCKER.
IN A PLAY, MY COUSIN,
FATHER'S BROTHER'S SON.

It is morning. I woke up to someone moving in my bed and found Julie snuggled up to me. When Dudi got up we decided to give each bunny a name: Pista, Erno, and Bandi. We all had breakfast and during the conversation she asked me why I don't ever invite Bandi over, and I told her that my mother won't allow it. She is not impressed by him: his parents are innkeepers. All the same, his older brother is already a university student. Later we went for a walk and met some boys whom Dudi knew from her previous visit to Miskolc. After dinner Julie went home to Hernadka to her parents'. Who knows if she was able to get a lift on a horse and cart or if she had to walk the seven kilometers?

The bunnies are here next to me. They are a lot of work, but they are very sweet. They leave their box constantly and have already walked around all five rooms. How do I know them by name? Well, Bandi has a black mark on its ear, Erno is the largest and the laziest, and the third is Pista the smallest. Today Dudi was telling me her experience was exactly the same as mine with the first boy she went out with and her mother objected to it. She is amazed that something could be so alike. Oh well, these mothers." Such is life" Dudi is leaving tomorrow by train, F. Laci will travel with her, so at least she won't be alone. The next day my mother returned from Kassa, and they just missed each other. Julie is also back from her visit to her parents', and evening mother goes with father to Budapest. I will stay alone here with Julie.

Next evening a couple of boys stopped by. We turned on the radio and again danced to the excellent jazz. At 11:00 p.m. they went home because they were sleepy. Julie is such a good English teacher that she spoke English even in her sleep.- I also had to study French. I have to go to my private teacher Boske, she gives me so much homework. Later I visited my girlfriend G. Juci. They own the largest shoe store in town. She told me that she would like to fall in love, it is time. "Sixteen years and never been kissed." (This is a well-known saying.) Her older sister Magda is married and has a baby girl. I love babies, and I told Magda I would be happy to take the baby with her carriage for a walk anytime. Her mother was home, and she told me that Bandi is a very pleasant, serious, well-brought-up boy. I wish my mother would have such an opinion of him. Mother arrived tonight with father, very elegant with a new spring coat and hat. She brought me a blouse, but it is too small for me. I guess she does not realize that I am still growing. When she heard that we had some boys in our home, she scolded me because it happened in their absence. At least Julie is very joyful and happy because she met a lot of boys from the Vasgyar (ironworks outside of Miskolc), and she keeps talking and talking. She is a lot of fun. She brings some gaiety into my life. It can be depressing being an only child.

1941. February 1. Saturday

And now I read what I wrote so far. I see myself so childish, so immature, that I wrote like this and I thought like this and how much more I changed. Bandi has been over since I met Francis while in Kassa on my vacation. He is older and more serious, and I saw the difference. But I don't want to write about him because in some time I will change again, like it happened with Bandi. I'd rather record something else.

I am in the 7th year of our school, the gimnazium; last month I turned 17 years old. My marks in math are much worse. This was never my favorite subject, but the mark I used to get was "good." This time I got a "satisfactory." I am very disappointed in myself. Everybody told me that I am a very talented kid, and I will be successful someday, but they are mistaken. Now when my only worries are the extra studies after school, this is my only duty, the languages and extra math, that I have to carry out. And what an easy task! Our professors are guiding us, and then after questioning they give us our marks. Where will this happen in life when one is working for oneself and has to be accountable only to oneself?! How will I be able to accomplish great assignments when now I am occupied from morning till evening and the result is...not much?

During the summer I was satisfied with myself. I moved around in a large social circle in Kassa, friends of my cousin Dudi, her age group. This of course did not demand any special knowledge, and there I held my own. But I did not see farther than my nose. I was told that I was very intelligent and I gladly accepted it. Where am I yet from Knowledge? How much more do I need to accomplish to call myself a person of culture? I had great goals ahead of me: I wanted to be a doctor. And meanwhile I realized that I was not capable and was too weak for this profession. Will I be the same as all the others: a marriage of convenience and raising children? Will I have even that much in my life in today's world, when all of Europe is in turmoil, when even the civilized world is damaging the best old fine arts with no consideration? They are bombing Milan—what will happen to the beautiful Gothic cathedral? How do I know about the cathedral? We have a wonderful art teacher in school who explains everything in an exciting way. She shows us pictures of the famous buildings and paintings with a projector on a screen. We are now already studying the Renaissance, how everything was concentrated in Firenze, Italy. This is the subject I like most. I hope someday I will be able to go there and see it for myself in person.

My father wanted to travel with me, and now I can be happy that I had a chance to see anything at all. What a nice trip we had on a ship down the Danube all the way to Varna in 1939. I was so proud that even though I was only 15 years old, he took me and not my mother. We met some nice people from

Budapest, and I became very friendly with two boys, one my age, Imre, and his older brother, Jozsi. Meeting them made the trip more fun. Also there was a very interesting man, a fashion designer who brought his phonograph with him. This is when I heard Ravel's *Bolero* the first time. He played it every day; I still have the music in my ears. He said that to design clothes for women is an art. To dress a young girl you don't need talent, you just pull a sack over her head and she looks good in it. I believe this to be true.

We stopped in Sofia, a very nice and very clean city, the capital of Bulgaria. And then we continued by train to Varna. The Bulgarians loved watermelon; they treated us on the train. Varna is a nice seaside resort on the Black Sea. This is where we stayed so my father could rest. We met some Hungarian marine cadets there, and as we talked to them about our life at home they told my father, "You should not go back to Hungary." Seems that they knew already then what will happen to the Jews as Hitler gets stronger. Of course he could not seriously think about that when he has an important job, a beautiful house, and is highly respected in the community.

One more thing. Before we left for the trip, my mother bought a lot of stockings and ladies' underwear to take with us. Her friends told her that there is a shortage in Bulgaria in women's lingerie, and we could sell it there for a good price. So when we arrived in Varna and we unpacked, my father looked at them and said no way will he try selling these things here. Now it was left to me what to do with it. I put it out nicely on the bed and called in the chambermaids. Even though I could not speak their language, I showed the pieces and wrote down the price, and in no time at all I sold everything.

It is possible that by the spring we will be at war too; we cannot tell what is awaiting us. To die so young? I love life and love living. My God, I am 17 years old. Yes, 17. How nice was my 16th year! I received everything I was waiting for: my dreams, dancing at the balls, success with the boys. Who knows what this year will bring?

1940 was a beautiful summer. My cousin Dudi (she is 2 years older than I am, and at this age that makes a big difference) was very popular among the young group. No wonder, she is very pretty, a real natural blonde, and has a very friendly personality. She took me along everywhere, even though I was younger than the others. When we went to the movies, we occupied a whole row. There were house parties, excursions in the neighboring woods, picnics, and visits to the city pool. I had none of this social life in Miskolc. My mother would not hear of it.

Francis, in labor camp, Slovakia 1941

Then upon coming home I heard that Francis (my friend from Kassa) was called into a labor camp in soldier's uniform but without guns.

This happened in all the towns with the Jewish boys. Soon my father went to a camp for three weeks in Hungary. How absurd, he is 51 years old. - Lory, the brother of Francis, is in Los Angeles now. Francis wanted to join him in

America where they have rich relatives, but the war prevented him from travel, even though he had all his papers prepared by then. This war has destroyed many things. Dudi would have married Lory; they were madly in love, and she would have gone with him to California, but her parents did not allow it.

That summer Julie was in Kassa with us and later Dudi came to us to Miskolc. We all got along so well. I think looking back sometime; I will be glad that I was together with Julie for so long. She is always cheerful; she brightens up the home. And not even mentioning the fact that both mother and I now speak English perfectly.Both Julie and I are teaching English, she for money and I teach Z. Zsuzsi in exchange for mathematics lessons. She is the best in class. I also teach mother French and Julie to play the piano.

1941 FEBRUARY 2. SUNDAY

I was interrupted here yesterday because Julie went to the ball and then we ate supper. This morning she came to my bed and she was talking and talking… She had a marvelous time, enjoyed great success. Her sister Gizi, who is older, chaperoned her. Now she is banging on the piano. She is very diligent, and in the end she will actually learn to play well. Later we went for a walk in my new winter outfit and new shoes. F. Gyorgy joined me. He danced with me the most during the ball, which was a week ago. I had a good time; it was nice that there was someone who paid attention to me. We talked a lot about books and girls, but now he was boring me. Besides, the new shoes were killing my feet, so we returned home.

1941. FEBRUARY 15, SATURDAY

My dad put on shoes for the first time after a long illness, and he and my mom went to play cards at the F. family's home. They had a big celebration—they had just bought a new house. They became very rich this year, like everyone who is self-employed, meaning that Mr. F. is not tied to an office like my dad. Actually there is a new urgency to purchase homes because prices are rising from one day to the next. They also raised the salaries at all the offices for everyone except for the Jews. Now I really feel the war; we have paper money instead of the pengo, the brass two filler (pence) was withdrawn, and the silver ten cents, which they reissued made of iron. They sell only one kind of bread or rolls. You can buy sugar with food stamps and only a certain amount of lard, (we cook with goose fat, so it doesn't concern us). All this increases the problems of running a household. People who have money are trying to get rid of it because it is losing its value by the day.

The Germans are crossing the country with tanks and automobiles moving south. The Italians suffered defeat in Africa by the English. Who knows what will yet develop here? We would like to sell the house on S. Street and buy a co-op in Budapest. Looks like my father will be fired in July anyway, and then it is better to be in Pest. But it is very difficult to execute this plan. There is terrific confusion and no time to contemplate all of it; on the other hand, the problem is to invest our money well, when nobody will give a guarantee that our money will be in a safe place. No one knows anything about our plan; we keep it a secret from Julie too, but maybe she suspects something. I would like to be already in Pest.

I have lot of conversations with Julie. She is so different from me when it comes to love. She would already go with some other boy if one does not call her for a week or two. I on the other hand, think of the future and of marriage if I like him. Which girl would not have these thoughts? I know Francis likes me. He is in love with me now, but I don't think that he needs me. I don't think he would want me for his wife, rather for his lover. All men want the same thing, and they all want to be the first. Yet only the husband has the right to be the first in a girl's life. Do we maybe we just have an exaggerated opinion of ourselves to give away our greatest treasure? None of them deserve it. Why is it truly such a treasure? And can anyone deserve it? If you know in advance that you will be sorry after, then don't do it—better that than to be filled with remorse. There are so many books I read about that…what problems are caused by indecision for every young girl. And the answer? Morals, purity, upbringing, honor. I think it is all up to the individual, and only afterward can you tell if you have made the right decision or not. There were stories when they could hold a man exactly with this, but more often it proved just the opposite. Why? Was the man disillusioned? Or simply that he got what he desired and he had no more to yearn for and got tired of it? Can it be that this is truly our greatest weapon? Nothing else counts: wit, culture, knowledge, and education are all dwarfed next to beauty? I have one real wish: a man who will love me; that is happiness, tranquility, and that can give value to life. Maybe I don't make much sense—one word contradicts the other—but it seems that everything is fermenting in me. I am going through a change, and I don't really know what I want.

Never has there been a more unpredictable future in front of youth as is now in front of us. I could just as well be poor and have a wretched existence all my life in this country as become a millionaire in America. Maybe I will find the true meaning of life and I will be very happy, but also it is possible that the happy, carefree life is behind me, while I did not even notice it, did not enjoy it, and the future holds nothing bright ahead of me. Can it be that I am afraid of the future, though I have no reason to be?

1941. April 25, Friday

I did not feel like writing for some time because something very sad happened, and it took me time to get over it. We had a change of maids, and mother hired a very nice young girl. She was pleasant and efficient, and we all liked her very much. She learned fast, and mother taught her to cook the way we liked it. Unfortunately not too long afterward she got ill—she was coughing a lot and when she did not get better, mother took her to our doctor, who diagnosed it to be tuberculosis. She had to go to the hospital. Mother visited her often and took her some food that she liked, but she was not getting better. It was shocking to me when she died—a girl so young, pretty, and healthy looking. Unfortunately in Hungary TB is widespread, and they have no cure for it. We heard about some families who had three or four children, and as they each reached 18 they died. Am I going to be in danger too?

As I took this booklet in my hand, made from such fine paper it is a delight while writing on it, my hand is caressing it. Truly, the papers made today because of this war are horrible! They turn yellow in comparison. But how silly I am to talk about such things when I did not sit down to write with this intention. Or is it possible at all to write a diary with a certain intention?

When writing a novel, I would know what I want to write about, at most the succession of the words develop according to my purpose. But in a diary? I write about whatever suddenly comes to mind. Or should I write perhaps a little history that is suitable to our infamous times, since surely posterity will remember this generation? Hmm. How great this is for us...

Our poor offspring will have to struggle with this too in school, learning in what month and on what Friday what Hitler occupied or people he conquered and what is contained in the first, second, or perhaps the third law constraining the Jews that is now hanging over our heads like the Sword of Damocles.

Yes we have a wonderful (horrible) state of affairs living through these historic times. We read the newspapers from morning to night and listen to the radio to learn what happens every minute. We study the map that is changing by the hour, wondering what are the German planes bombing now, or what did the German troops occupy, because the British are only powerful through the radio airwaves and blare their strength all over the world. But to act forcefully? No. They are either weak or cowardly. Basically we watch this day after day, and we are wasting all our lives worrying so that someday the future generation would remember these words: Hitler conquered the World.

But I think I wrote enough about politics; let the historians and scholars talk about this. I don't feel that I belong to them. So what am I really? A simple student who, being a Jew, may not be able to graduate. Here at home considered a stupid child who makes no sense, it is almost hopeless; before my teachers, an ambitious kid; and I, judging myself, a grown, serious woman, who is not afraid of the future, who feels strength in herself facing anything and everything, and who willingly takes on life's great battles. So here you are—you may choose. That I became a bit cynical is understandable; in this world it can happen in the best of families. That I am a pessimist is old news, and that I am very much alone is a universal human attribute that can't be helped. And to all the boys I met so far, where are you with these problems, how could you understand me to be my good friends, and how could you love me so that I should not feel so lonely?

1941. JUNE 16, MONDAY

Today is my mother's birthday. I bought a nice bouquet of roses, and she is going out to dinner with father. I got a visitor today. Zsuzska, my cousin from Ungvar, arrived. She came by train, and father went to pick her up at the station. Mostly we see each other in Kassa—she seldom comes down to us. I already planned our activities for how to spend our days together. When the weather is nice, and it should get warm by now, we will go to the strand, —the spa that belongs to the Electric Trust Company, where my father is the director. My girlfriends will be there, and we may meet some of the boys too. On the weekend we will go to the Bukk Mountain on the small train, D. Imre will be leading us through the woods; he knows every path and never gets lost. Zsuzska just mentioned that she looks forward to having a campfire, and there we will fry bacon and then drip the grease on bread. She still remembers this from last time she was here; it was so delicious. In Ungvar she goes to a Hebrew gimnazium, but at home they speak Hungarian. They also study English in school, which will be very helpful now that she can speak with Julie a little.

And I will not feel so lonely while she is with us.

1941. OCTOBER 11, SATURDAY

I wrote quite a while ago, didn't I? Though I wanted to many times since, I was either not in the mood or I could find no time. Or when I had both, I was not alone. Now I have all three, and I'll do my best to take advantage of it. I am trying to rise above this small bourgeois life, having no goal to reach, the fight for the daily bread (not even bread and butter as the English say) without any larger, higher, more-esteemed, stimulating thoughts. I'm so afraid if in the end I will reach the lifestyle my mother and her friends live: in a nice family circle, merely filled with the problems of housecleaning and laundry, the biggest worry what to cook tomorrow and that you have to buy material for dresses now because later you won't be able to find pure wool anymore.

I entered my eighth and final year. I reached this year when it is truly only one step into LIFE. I don't like the school; I don't like the class, the girls, the professors. I don't like the atmosphere I am in, because I cannot be successful; I feel stifled, not because they are superior but perhaps they are more aggressive or luckier. Yes I am too vain to accept this third-rate role of a chambermaid—would it be possible that all my life I will be only a little amateur? Perhaps I overrate myself? This is possible, but I may need to do that even more so in order to stand out.

If in today's world I cannot be a doctor because the new law brought in *numerus nullus*, meaning that Jews cannot enter the universities, I would like to become an operating nurse. So far I did not know if I would have enough strength of mind for it. But this summer I had the chance to watch two operations. It was super! My pediatrician, whom I have outgrown by now, was very nice to me, and when he heard that I would like to go to the hospital to see an operation close by, he arranged for me to go with him. I got a white coat and was introduced as a Medica. I guess I must have looked like one because I faced no objections. I saw a caesarean, which was most exciting. The mother was under anesthesia. They cut her stomach open and lifted out the baby, who was then taken by the nurse and started to cry at once. A real miracle of nature. Also on another patient I witnessed the removal of part of a cancerous stomach. I was very attentive and did not faint, so I proved that I could be a surgeon if I had the chance. And here I know I could be somebody, and the doctors would appreciate me more than my classmates. I would feel that I have a role in life. I am not only an "extra"—I am important. When will I actually get there and at what cost?

Will there be a time when I will look back on life as Professor Tarzay, with a strong sarcastic line around her mouth? With so much knowledge, well versed in so many subjects, and with memories of sorrow and disappointments and yet still happy?

I am always in a hurry. It's my fault that I could never wait patiently for something to happen. The clock is running, the days are rolling by, and I wonder whether I have used my years to the best advantage. Would I do things differently if I could do it over again? Yes, without question. I would never abandon Agi. with whom my mother spoiled our relationship. We went to the park in the afternoon, and I did not tell mother about it. Agi was with me and we met some boys, but when mother asked us she denied it too, trying to protect me. Mother called her in her room, closed the door so I would not hear her, and I have no idea what she could have told her to alienate her from me forever. I would still have a real good friend, I would have a warm contact in my life who would love me and who I could always depend on. But this is needless speculation. Now, I cannot change my past and I do not know my future. Pity that I am not like the others. I would not have to always analyze my life, and I could be satisfied, since even though I have so much and have received so much, why can't I appreciate it? Can I then expect that others should appreciate me?

Agi, my best friend.

CHAPTER II

1941. NOVEMBER 5, WEDNESDAY

There is a Puccini evening on the radio, and when I hear his music somehow I always have a desire to write. I don't know why music has such an influence on me, but at a time like this I feel capable to reach everything: greatness, beauty, an all-time prominence. I wonder why? After all, there are such turning points in a person's life, such events that are so much more important that they are of a greater influence in the formation of the future than such a Puccini evening. Still at that time I *don't* feel that I must write it down...later I will have to see it on paper. Is it perhaps because those things we never forget anyway?

That's how it happened with Francis. I broke up with him a few weeks ago, and not once did I get to write about it. It was all very strange. My thoughts cooled toward him, and I realized that he was not for me. Yes, I agreed with Gyuri that I need more than a thousand other girls, that I strive to higher goals where Francis could not lead me. (He could not even follow me.) Now I am free. I am not longing for anyone; I do not miss anyone but Gyuri. Yes, I miss terribly those discussions that were so refreshing and could make me feel so happy. Well I am not unhappy now because I study preparing for my graduation. I don't want to finish with a "satisfactory" mark, so all my days are spent on school work.

Gyuri, Miskolc 1941.

Once a week I go to a movie and relax, feel mentally refreshed, and get into a good mood. I don't mean that I am in a bad mood now, but at that time I am definitely in good humor. The world they show in the movies is so different, full of possibilities, artistic talents, and splendidly eventful lives. Will mine ever be like that? Will I look back on my past so that I will be able to search and choose among my many memories? I wish it were like that. That is why I study diligently because I would like to get the most of what school can offer me since I have only this, the last year now. They say a person reads and learns the most up to the age of 18. I would not like it to be so, and I will not allow it to be so. There is such great knowledge ahead of me that I want to work through and that cannot be denied me. Possibly we will move up to Budapest; however, even without my parents, I would still like to go. But I cannot allow that the same thing should happen to me as with the other girls, to live only for amusements, entertainment. It is nice to enjoy some entertainment, but it should be selective and serious. It's true I will not even have a lot of time, but I don't want to fear myself. I want to be sure of myself. It would be so good to have Gyuri here with me, to help me, yet I don't dare to turn to him. I'm afraid he would love me like he loved me before, when he wrote those beautiful poems to me and I know that I could not return such great love. I cannot be so selfish that I should not care about his life. It was so nice to discuss everything with him. Discuss? We always had the same opinion. But actually because of that it felt so good to talk about them with a sympathetic soul. Now I see that this is what I miss, nothing else. So I leave the boys. I am better off without them.

Budacker, our principal, would say, "My child, there are so many questions which arise in your soul, have faith and God will give you the answer." Poor man. But still it is good for him; he is surely contented.

I now read some sections of what I wrote so far, and there I expressed that I should be alone and study diligently in the remaining time. And now I see that without reading all this, I have accomplished just that. Nevertheless my smarter being, my rational self, triumphed. Does this show that I am getting older? And I am not the only one changing that much. F. Lilli broke up with her boyfriend now (well it's because she has a new one). F. Jutka put an end to meeting D. Imre because she is also driven by ambition to study. My mom is right: "All of you have come to your senses." When I was 15 and 16 I thought I was a big girl. Am I a big girl now? There will be a time when I will smile at myself. In fact there will always be such a time. From a distance one can always see even one's own actions more objectively.

1942. January 15, Thursday

I just wrote a camp postcard to my father. He has now been in Sianki, Poland, for three weeks, in a labor camp, in the winter, in the snow and cold. He is 52 years old. There because of professional jealousy? For sure there was someone malicious who

Sianki, Father at age 52, labor camp 1942.

wanted his job or his salary or God only knows what and had him called into the military and to a labor camp. Yes, today this can be done too, to get rid of someone because he has an important high position and is a Jew. We are living in the times when anything is possible—things we could not even imagine before and this is what the world comes to. On Tuesday the draft arrived, Wednesday he had already left for Kassa, mom with him, and by Thursday morning one soldier with a gun took him away. Mother came home with the news that they took dad to

Galicia from where no one came back alive. My heart stopped. I ran to school so that I could talk to Henkey, my classmate.

It is interesting that there are things that you cannot know in advance. At the start of classes, I wanted to sit next to my friend Zsuzsi, but F. Jutka already preceded me. I was so angry with her! By chance I was seated next to Henkey, whose father is a general. She took me to her father. I was crying, begging that my father cannot go to Galicia, this should not happen, he must do something. And then I was running with mother from person to person searching for every straw I could grab onto, and all that meant nothing. My father is still there shoveling snow, but we at least know that he is alive—that he is relatively well and he writes us regularly.

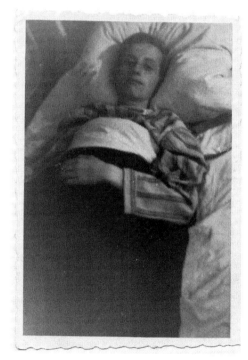

Otti, on his deathbed after ski accident as soon as we arrived

Life is unpredictable. I became fatalistic—I, who always trusted only myself and chance, which may slip by or be caught in time. Fate, destiny? Ridiculous! I would have said a month ago and now that is the only explanation I find for everything; this is how it had to happen. For the Christmas holidays mother and I went to Kassa to our family. She had to rest a bit, and it did not hurt me either to relax. The four days we spent there were very pleasant, getting away from it all. By New Year's Eve we were back home, and we spent the night with the F. family and our social circle, whom we are friendly with here in Miskolc. I enjoyed myself and was glad that at least one evening was very nice. This was Wednesday.

On Saturday morning we received a letter from Kassa. Otti (Dudi's younger brother) had a ski accident; he broke his spine, and he will have an X-ray done on his back. We called them by phone that evening, and talked to Uncle Gyula. The spine broke, and the spinal cord separated—poor boy would be better off not to stay alive. Sunday we left for Kassa. The train is only a few hours from Miskolc.

As soon as we arrived we went to the hospital, and from this day on every day for a week at eight in the morning, I walked this road in the dark. When later his head started healing, he recognized me and kissed me again and again. He looked so nice lying there with his cheeks flushed from fever, with his golden curly hair, looking strong and healthy when in fact the poor boy could not even move. He is paralyzed below the waist. Would I have believed in God, for sure I would have lost my faith now. What crime did this poor sixteen-year-old child commit? He who would have just started truly living and could have enjoyed life.

Enjoy life? Can anyone enjoy life, which holds out promises every minute, but instead of delights and pleasures, only new troubles, worries, and a desperate, hopeless future? Yet as long as man is living, he has hopes, waiting that all will change, will get better; after all it cannot stay like this forever! Yes, he hopes while he is healthy. But what hope can a poor boy, paralyzed, have, who cannot yet look back in the past and who does not have a future? And what sin did that poor father and mother commit that fate should strike them like this? Is there a God who, after weighing all things, would thus consider to direct the life of the individual this way? Is there any justice in the heavens? What do we expect then from fallible men to be fair and just when the Higher Power is not?

So this is how I spent my vacation. And I still cannot regain my composure. I will never be the same again as I was three weeks ago. Somehow I feel that I got older. Yes, there is in me a very deep-seated sadness that I try to hide. I try to smile, but all in vain; the smile freezes on my face, and I slip back unintentionally into this sad mood again. Somehow I watch the other girls from afar, as if I were not of the same age with them but at least ten years older.

I will be 18 in two days. What a birthday! Mother is in Budapest for a checkup at the doctors because she has gallstones, and my poor father wrote me only one letter, and as many times as I read it I must cry. All reason doesn't count now: Magda, you cannot get anywhere with reason only; you have to be strong emotionally, for there are some difficult ordeals in life ahead.

This is my first birthday that I do not spend with my parents. Just the thought brings a feeling of tightness in my throat, especially during such circumstances. When one arrives at such a milestone, one usually looks back on the bygone year. This time last year I looked back on my 16th birthday, which was very happy, but the 17th already was a difficult year, and it ended in sorrow.

I wonder what 1942 will bring. Can anything even worse exist, or from now on can better things follow? I bury myself in my work from six in the morning till ten at night; at least during this time I stop contemplating. But I think I detect a weakness here. I am not what I was hoping to be. I cannot live alone without affection, especially not in such difficult times. I feel so much love in me, and I have no one to share it with, one who would be happy to receive it. I know it is smart and right the way I am behaving now, yet I feel that something is missing in my life. The true purpose is something that fills one's entire soul, every minute, subconsciously every thought. In vain do I delude myself, in vain do I train myself, educate myself, in vain I am in eighth year, in vain I yearn to have peace in the family. Still I am a woman. I am 18 years old—if now I do not enjoy the better side of life (if there is such a thing at all), when will I?

Oh God, Destiny, Luck, Chance, Providence, Nature…give me a happy 18th year!

1942. SEPTEMBER 26, SATURDAY BUDAPEST

I turned 18 years old. Indeed I graduated and received my diploma.

GRADUATION 1942 In our classroom of 8 years, Magda 3rd row on left

Another summer passed, my dad returned home, and we moved to Budapest. This is all that happened with me in a nutshell. Zsuzsa is already engaged; her wedding will be in October. The others are sewing, F. Jutka goes to Zion, R. Juci is learning to be a cosmetician, and I am teaching English.

Well I have to write a bit more about what happened before we left Miskolc in June. Most important, mother went to Kassa—and with a lot of money, I never learned how much, but she managed to get my father back to the hospital, where he stayed until we moved to Buda. They did buy an apartment in Pest a year ago and rented it thinking that when they are ready they will move there. Yes, but there entered a new ordinance: you could not put out a tenant unless you can offer an equal home for them, which of course was an impossibility. So my parents found a nice apartment in Buda for us. After my graduation mother and I packed up our house, forty-four wooden crates and the furniture, as much as we could use in the new apartment, and father was able to come to join us in Bajvivo street without ever returning to Miskolc. People thought "he smells the violets from below," of course meaning he is underground, which is what we wanted them to believe. He had lost twenty kilo, but he was well and finally back with us. Yes, but this experience had a very heavy influence on his attitude, his outlook on life; he was heartbroken, and his whole world had collapsed around him. Here he was living like a fugitive, robbed from his prestigious position that he had worked for all his life, in an apartment in Buda without even being able to say good-bye to his beautiful home in Miskolc and his lifelong friends. He lacked the vitality to start anew, and mother and I did not know how to help him.

As for my graduation, we were ten Jewish girls in a class of forty, most of them good students, but as much as I excelled, they found a way to spoil my grades. We wore a Bocskay uniform with a cap, and one day when I was walking with Julie on Szechenyi Street, Budacker saw me without my cap. I only found out about this the next week when the headmaster came to our class and together with Budacker read out loud my warning of poor conduct, which of course spoiled my overall grades. I became hysterical, ran out of the class crying, and slammed the door behind me. They actually got alarmed that I would do something to myself and sent one of the girls after me. This was something unheard of, another slap in the face, a reminder of the Nazi era this time touching me personally.

Budapest is beautiful, but alone I cannot enjoy it enough. The fact is that I am very much alone. Today I went to the Palatinus on Margarite Island. They call it a "beach," with many swimming pools, soft, well-kept lawn, and lots of people— children and lovers who are sunning and enjoying a beautiful day. September was never as nice as now. It looks like people are not concerned about the war.

In Miskolc they are drafting a lot of men; friends of my father were sent to labor camps and died while sweeping for mines. Budapest has been bombed twice since we have been here. Our air-raid shelter is good, nice and new. We live in a six story building. I do not miss Miskolc; I was pretty lonely there too. There is no hope to meet a man; they were all drafted, and the twenty-one year olds are leaving now. I met a few boys from home, but they are all preoccupied. We have to try to enjoy every day while we are still around, healthy and well.

They did not accept me in the university, not even for a dietician. I cannot enter an Italian course because I am Jewish, and if my student would find this out she would probably leave me. It's a bitter life. I left Julie in Miskolc, so now I have no one to complain to.

It is a good feeling to be able to earn enough money independently, so I don't have to ask my parents for every penny I need, however I cannot enjoy this either. Zsuzsa was born to be happy; I, instead, am only searching for happiness. And I still could not accept that Otti is dead. When Uncle Joska comes to visit us I have it on my tongue to ask, "And Otti?" But of course I kept quiet. I think Dudi forgets easier—she is a strange girl; she has no heart, all egoism. I cannot even believe all the horrors that I hear. Better not to think about it, not to think at all, live only for today. Beautiful Budapest, the city of lights, is in the dark. We go to bed now at 9:30. This is no life for a young girl. I won't even write anymore because I don't want to be contemplating, anyway I am not in a talkative mood. I'll be writing next time.

1942. NOVEMBER 29, SUNDAY

I wrote in my diary months ago, though I would have liked to write many times since, but I was never alone. Just now I have a greater need for my diary because Julie is not here with me. I have no one to whom I can tell everything, and I am even more alone than ever before. However I cannot complain. My father is at home, which today is a special happiness. And I have a girlfriend, R. Juci, also from Miskolc, who moved to Budapest a few years ago, and she continued her schooling here in the capital. Also if I would want to I could have four to five more friends, although I cannot say that no one is courting me. There is a young man, N. Tibor, a law student, 21 years old, a brat, a typically rich boy from Budapest. He is not my type, but at least I am going places, I meet people, and today you cannot be too choosy. Outside of the 20 year olds, nobody is at home anymore.

There are always more men without legs and arms. There is always less bread and more problems, they darken the city earlier, and there are more and more accidents. People queue up in more places, and you can get more things only for coupons—or sometimes not even for coupons anymore. And all this is dragging on; the war does not want to end, though it would be about time.

My girlfriend Zsuzsi in Miskolc got married, and the next day they took her husband away; they could not even have a wedding at the temple. Wherever you look there is no happiness. Today there are no love affairs, no happy engagements or weddings; today people are not glad to have a child because there are more disadvantages than advantages trying to bring them up. Only with Gyuri can I have a pleasant conversation; he is the nicest young man whom I now know. He is here in Budapest, working hard in a textile factory, but he is so good natured, it does not bother him. He is always in a good mood, always joking. I wish I would have half as much merriment and good humor in my nature.

I attend a school for shorthand and typing three times a week in the mornings, and the homework takes up the rest of my time. I go out every evening somewhere because I simply cannot stay at home. It is too depressing here—the atmosphere makes me nervous. I have no patience to read, I don't play the piano—actually I don't know what I want and what is the matter with me. If I could redo every day that goes by, I would do it differently.

Yesterday we were with Tibor's friend and the girl he is going with, in other words, a foursome. It is possible that they had a good time, but I was deathly bored and I had only one thought:

Was this worth something? Did I need this? Did I receive anything by all this? I was in the theater twice. The shows were weak, the actors fabulous. At least this gives you something to think about. Still to this day my favorite entertainment is the movies; they are what offer the most.

I also went to three concerts. I got acquainted with a violinist, Tamas, and it was he who took me to a few concerts. I was not familiar with the music, and I did not enjoy the evening as much as the concerts at home in Miskolc. When someone came down from Budapest, I was enthusiastic about it; I could abandon myself completely to the music, and I was crying with it and laughing with it. But now I listen like a sober outsider, the crowd is disturbing to me, as well as the elegance, the lights, and the mental attitude. Perhaps it is also that Tamas is sitting next to me and that I have to watch every movement of mine, every gesture, and that I cannot act natural even for a moment. I seem to be like this in front of everyone these days.

Tamas, violinist in Budapest 1942

Of course I like the idea that I can be with someone the press is writing about, whom people are interested in. I am also pleased that this Thursday I will go to his concert. then among the hundreds of people who will be sitting there listening to him, I will be one who has some personal contact with him and who goes backstage to congratulate him. Yes, all this is pleasing to my vanity; it is good to tell my girlfriends that I will go to the movies with Tamas tomorrow—that Tamas whom they know only from the posters. Tibor does not know that we meet; he only knows about him. Once he said that he is not jealous at all because he knows I am only one of his admirers. This remark felt insulting to me then, but now I see he was right. If I would be closer together with Tamas, I would be only a matchstick in his life. When he lights it, he enjoys the flame, but when the fire fizzles out, he throws it away and forgets it the same minute. Well, I will not be that flaming matchstick.

Last time I wrote, I was not happy because I had so much love in me, and I had no one to share it with. And now I noticed that I no longer have such great love in me. Is it gone? Did it vanish? I feel that I could not love anyone now. Whether I miss this or not, I don't know. Will I be able to love anyone who would fill all my thoughts again, one who would enrich my every minute and would embellish my dreams? I hope so.

1942. December 25, Friday

It is the night of Christmas. I'm sitting here, and from London a divine jazz is flowing through me with a heartbreaking mellow crooning male voice. And I am alone. It is Christmas again, another year gone by. It did not bring anything, nothing nice, nothing new, nothing worthwhile to remember. Only more sadness. Perhaps I am more level headed. The music is crying "La Paloma." I would also be in the mood to cry, but I try to be strong, cannot get upset about everything. The desire to go places, which was driving me when we came to Budapest, has slowly died out. All week I did not go anywhere. I stay home reading, working with my stamp collection, and practicing shorthand and typing. I'm helping with the housework and am learning to cook and bake; this is how my days go by. I do not meet anyone, and I don't miss anyone.

During the holiday the streets are quiet, though there is a festive mood inside the lobby of the movie houses. There are beautiful Christmas trees decorated with electric candles. But this is a black Christmas; I cannot enjoy sparkling snow crunching under my feet. I miss Miskolc and Patak street, where I crossed every morning with schoolbag in my hand, Bocskay cap on my head, and, in a dark blue coat and under my ugly, high, brown student shoes the fresh tall snow was crackling. My face flushed from the cold, and around me all the girls with equally flushed faces were joyfully moving on to school. This picture appears to me as if it were so long ago, floating in front of my eyes, but it is still sharp and clear like that sunny winter morning. On two sides I see the old sumac trees, to the right the winding, dirty Pece Creek, which at this time would be completely frozen. I can almost hear behind the fence the barking dog. And I don't know why, but I peek into a window with my psychic eyes, where an old brass owl sits on the desk with spread wings. This was Gyuri's former room. How long ago it was that he moved from there, but I still looked in every morning. From habit? Or did I expect him all at once to greet me, smiling like long ago? I don't know. Every hour of this Christmas hurts me, and I cannot even imagine that I will have a pleasant New Year's Eve, and then a better year, a nicer year will follow..

The university shortened the medical faculty with one year. It will take one less year to graduate. Oh God, if by spring the war would end and I could study to be a doctor! That would be too beautiful; I don't even dare to dream about it. Perhaps I could even go abroad to England or America, and I could study there. I would not even lose more than one year, and since now it only will last four years...No, no I don't even think about it. Gyuri always told me that I should never give up my goal because one cannot live without a purpose. He is right. My life today is not living. I don't study, I don't get ahead. Only time is flying and I stand still. I cannot even write anymore.

1943. January 29, Friday

The New Year is here. It started quite well. I was with my parents in the Community Center, which had a good program. After that we toasted the New Year with Tokaj Aszu.

In the following days I got to know a distant relative of ours, W. Gyorgy and with him and his friend we went to the Hungaria Hotel and the next day to the Ritz for five o'clock tea. These two days were very enjoyable. I got a little taste of how life would be if we lived in a normal world, and the young men would be home. But then they left.

One of Dudi's friends from Kassa came to visit us, and he took me to the Arizona nightclub and also to the Gellert Hotel for five o'clock tea, and then to the movies. With other words I had plenty of entertainment. And meanwhile I turned 19 years old. I'm glad the 18th is over; it was an ugly year. Perhaps this year will be more eventful? I feel that now even at home they accepted me as a grown-up girl. I got a fabulous nutria fur coat, and mother took me to the top salon on the Vaci Street to Clara Rothschild to have a nice black silk dress made for me. I am elegant, and wherever I go people stare at me, men and women both. Now I know that I am pretty, I see that I am pretty. I was always thinking how lucky beautiful women are; every time they look in the mirror they can admire themselves, their beauty. Now I feel this too, and it is good to look in the mirror when a nice young girl looks back at me. However I am preoccupied with the thought that my children should also be good looking, even nicer and not less than I am. There is nothing worse than to see the mother of my girlfriend, young and radiant, and her daughter is not. How can I choose a husband so that my children should be beautiful? Is this my disadvantage that I am attractive? I am not occupied enough with studies, books, science, and the arts. Mom does not want me to study too much, and I don't find the time for it now anyway. The boys are complimenting me, but I would prefer to have a candid talk with someone intelligent and cultured like I used to have with Gyuri.

We are getting some news from the front. Finally the Russians beat back the Wehrmacht attacks in Leningrad. This may have tremendous consequences psychologically. Winter there is so horribly cold, and the Germans could not stand it for so long.

Magdi, the older sister of Gyuri, called me and she told me that Gyuri is in the hospital. They operated on his legs for varicose veins. I could only think that when they call him into the military perhaps he felt that he would not be able to march any distance. I never heard him talk about this before. I went to visit him, and I met Stella, who was sitting next to his bed. Who is Stella? That's not important, but three time a day she sits next to him, takes care of him, and entertains him. They "tutoyer" (speaking informally) Gyuri, and I never did. And he loves her, cares for her and worries about her, teaches her, and enjoys her constant smile, her gaiety, and her free and feminine style.

Wednesday I went there again. I sat with him all afternoon and then I felt that I have nothing to do here anymore. Here the doors are closed to me; they are not happy to see me, and I do not mean as much to him now as before. Stella ran in for only a minute. She brought a newspaper for Gyuri, but that minute meant more to him than my presence during the whole afternoon. It hurts me deeply when I think of it, but this was my fault. I let my luck pass by me, unnoticed. And now I must learn to forget, since after all this I don't even dare to talk to Gyuri. Why should the past force itself onto the present? Perhaps Stella needs him even more than I do. So I will have to forget.

We now heard on the radio for the first time that the Americans were bombing Germany. It is about time that they should seriously intervene in this war. The British captured Tripoli from the Italians, and we are sitting here watching from the sidelines, waiting to see what will happen next. So far our life continues the same way, and there are no drastic changes.

My mother doesn't feel well; her gallbladder causes her a lot of pain. In times like this she stays in bed because it weakens her very much and the doctors are suggesting an operation, but she cannot make a decision to undergo such a drastic solution.

1943. May 6, Thursday

Tuesday mother was operated on at the private Fasor Sanatorium; they removed her gallbladder, which was full of stones. Professor Adam is a very clever doctor. Mother was wheeled into the operating room at noon, and she was already out at one o'clock smiling as if nothing had happened. Thank God she feels well; at last all the worries are over. In the last weeks she had attacks so often that she was in bed more than on her feet. She could not do anything, and everything tired her, so in the end she got fed up with it and finally made up her mind to have the operation. Of course now dad and I are with her all day. We engaged a nurse to be with her for the first two nights, but tonight she will be on her own. She is in a double room, and by coincidence a very likable woman from Miskolc is next to her. Her daughter attended the teacher's college, and I suggested that we could open an English nursery school. Not a bad idea, and we will talk more about it, but it is very difficult to find a location. It would be good if I could find a solution to a more substantial income. At present teaching English privately is only enough for pocket money.

Meanwhile I went for a few days to a copy-typist office from 8:30 a.m. to 1:30 p.m. I got two pengo per day, which is ridiculous, however it would have been worthwhile to continue so I would get the hang of it. But the office did not do well—they did not have enough work, so they did not need me. I applied for some other jobs, but so far there is nothing. Actually it is better that I don't have full-time employment because I am cleaning, cooking, and washing the dishes (cannot get a maid). I am visiting mom in the hospital, and I am giving lessons. I have no time for anything, I am way behind with my correspondence, and I don't even have the time to take care of my own personal things, like my stockings. Of course this week I did not have any opportunities for entertainment anyway.

Last Sunday I went to Visegrad with Gyuri for the whole day.

**Visegrad on the Danube,
Magda, May 1943**

A boat goes up there on the Danube. It was a very pleasant trip and it was a beautiful sunny day, just like you would expect in May. I took the first step when I finally could not wait any longer, and sent him a letter and asked simply why he did not call on me, why he did not give any sign of how he felt. I had the courage to write everything I thought. I needed to do that. Now at least we could play with our cards on the table. And he returned to me with more affection than before, because now we appreciate each other and love each other with pure, tranquil, happiness, not with raging passion. We do not exchange gushing words, we will not meet every day, and we do not demand anything from each other. We know that we exist, that we will exist for each other always, and that this is a very good feeling for both of us. Meanwhile he goes out with Stella, because she needs him now, and I am also with other boys. I don't want my mother to talk (as she always does if I am interested in any boy). It feels good that I make an impression on them; they are looking for my company and I enjoy their attention.

I meet Tamas quite often since he was released from the military. Yet when I am daydreaming, it is always Gyuri I am thinking of, not Tamas. It would be so nice, so peaceful, so comfortable, to live my life next to Gyuri. It would not be boring, monotonous, or average; there is something calming in him, something interesting, unlike with others. I also meet G. Pista, but I don't really like him. His parents are rich merchants in Kassa, which is what my mother likes so much, but I am not at all interested in commerce. Same as with P. Gyorgy, who always compliments me and who has such a "mother-in-law" mother. Actually the fact is that my father was a colleague of his father in the Trust in Budapest. When we lived in Miskolc and we sometimes went to Budapest, my father for business, mother and I shopping, we always visited his parents in their home. But let's drop this marriage talk; it is useless to speculate.

For now I study. I just started German shorthand, but it really is not to my liking. It is tedious, and it would take a long time to learn. Most upsetting is that I do not play the piano. I really have no time for it. But it would be a pity to forget what I know.

During Easter I was planning to go to the Bukk Mountains. I was longing to walk in the woods, enjoy the solitude, relax and get away from it all, but I could not go because mother did not feel well and our maid left us. Now I decided to go hiking in the neighboring woods in Budapest every Sunday, and I find that this makes up for the Bukk somewhat. This Sunday was also beautiful, and I really enjoyed it.

Since we moved to Budapest, my mother stopped keeping a kosher home. While my grandmother lived and sometimes visited us in Miskolc, mother wanted to be sure that she would have confidence to eat at our home. During Passover we cleaned the house thoroughly; every corner was swept so no bread crumbs would remain anywhere. We changed the dishes and took the pots and pans and other utensils to the orthodox section of Miskolc where they "koshered" them. I remember they stuck the knives in the ground, and the next day we went to pick them up after the rabbi inspected them. The Seder was celebrated according to tradition. I read the Hagada, and father leaned back on a pillow, as it was written, and we ate only matzos for the whole week. But after what we have gone through with the war and grandmother is no more, all that has lost its significance and importance.

Ah yes, the war? It has no intention to end. Who knows how long it will last and how will we recover from it? I wish that it should never get worse than it is now. I would already settle for the status quo. I wish they would not call Gyuri into the military for quite some time.

1943. MAY 17, MONDAY

ONE DAY IN VISEGRAD
1943 MAY 3rd.

Noble and long standing Master!
Painter coating ancient canvases,
From the beginning of Quattrocento,
Lover of soft, clean colors,
Take a glance for a moment I beg you,
From behind your white ruffled sky,
With humble, knowledgeable eyes,
With your Godly seeing sight,
Observe the region of Visegrad,
That spreads about the Castle.

The sky is a pale blue ethereal veil,
Light green is the bordering meadow
While below the Duna flows unnoticed
Under the leafy boughs which bloom,
Maestro, dare I ask,
Would you paint your Madonna there?
Bathing in the splendor of May,
May brightened our spirit,
Birds were singing for us
And in return we sang to the birds,

The flower scented breeze was kissing us
The breeze with its gentle arms embraced us,

Like sweet dreams were your countless kisses,
Walking, running arm in arm,
And we were pure like children,
As everything was clean and pure
The two of us among trees, grass and flowers,
Only two of us and the Great God.

Shall we listen to the birds twitter,
Will this May remain ours,
With the breeze and the scent of flowers?
And this town with its cold walls
Will not tear our hands apart,
Our lips and our love,
Will always remain with us Great God?

Old Master, do not blend your colors,
Oh, this cloud will be too dark,
Leave it, please, I beg you, leave it white,
Innocent like the child,
Who is lying so tenderly
In the lap of your sweet Madonna,
Leave the cloud I beg you, pristine and white
Above all allow our love to be, let it live, let it thrive!

What do I want to write about? Gyuri sent me a poem, which he wrote when we were in Visegrad. This is what I must write about because I am happy, so much so that I cannot keep it to myself. I must write it down since I cannot tell anybody. I finally found myself, my peace and quiet. I do not chase after anything, neither entertainment nor work nor study. I don't have to immerse myself into anything to try to forget, to not think, because I truly like to think—I want to think. It feels good, and it makes me happy. And for all this I can thank Gyuri, whom I finally found and who is mine, whom I subconsciously was always looking for. He is the one who helps me out, who is my equal and makes me complete, who loves me and whom I love.

This is something other than what I had with Bandi or Francis; I don't even call that "love" because this is completely different and much more than that. It is not stormy and does not cause problems; instead, it is soothing and solves all problems. The very best I feel now is a peace and quiet that I cannot explain. And it is good that I do not speak about it to anyone because it would become dull; I must not put it into spoken words because others would not understand it anyway. I think of Gyuri every minute: what there was and what there is and a lot about what it would be if it could remain like this forever...I have never felt this before. With Bandi we were making plans with childish ideas, but secretly I always felt that this is only a game, nothing serious, yet I did not want to be the one to spoil it. As for Francis, I have never planned for the future, but now each time I am with Gyuri my imagination runs ahead.

The other day Gyuri came to visit our home. I have served him supper as if it were the most natural daily occasion and I "saw" that it will always be like this later, when we will be only the two of us in the apartment, and that apartment will be ours. When he sat in the armchair and I settled down on the arm next to him; I felt with a sure and undeniable feeling that this moment will repeat itself one day, when I will be his wife. I fear to write down this word, as if I would say it too soon and fate would lead my life toward a different way for being too presumptuous—that this should not happen in spite of it all and I should not be happy.

I feel that together we could be very happy; we understand each other so well, and we love each other so much. Would it be possible that the war would end by autumn and Gyuri would be able to work and be a success and be discovered and be recognized and have a name and that my mother would also be pleased to have a "good catch" because only then would they marry off their only daughter, and all this would happen in three or four years so we can live happily ever after?! We then would have children, smart, talented, and pretty, whom it will be worthwhile to work and to live for. And that the two of us would love each other for ever, with happy heavenly love. Could this be possible? I don't know how it will be from here on, or what will happen if he will be drafted. I am so terribly afraid to lose him.

A couple days ago when I was walking with Gyuri, we met Tamas on the street. I blushed dreadfully. This encounter was unusual, and a lot of things passed through my mind and rolled down in front of my eyes in that minute while he tipped his hat and I returned his greeting. So here they were at the same time next to each other, together the two contrasts, which I could separate so well from each other but which somehow I did not wish to bear together. Tamas is always so charming, praising me; he is flattering and courting me and is never critical toward me. With every word he makes me feel how much I appeal to him. On the other hand, Gyuri is quiet, as if he would see nothing and does not feel it important to let me know what he does observe, and with this he prevents me from ever gaining the upper hand over him or that I would become conceited.

Tamas bargains with me that I have time to go home since it is only nine thirty and I am truly a big girl now, and Gyuri wants to see me home with no objections. But in any case I love Gyuri, I respect him, think highly of him and I look up to him. Gyuri is 22 years old and Tamas is 30. When I am with Tamas, it is very pleasant to be with him, very entertaining, but if I am with Gyuri I feel at every occasion that I received something and that I can live on this something for weeks. I am lying and using tactics with Tamas, but to Gyuri I am as candid as to myself and...the big difference is that I have a good time with Tamas, but I love Gyuri.

1943. June 7, Sunday

It is five weeks since I was in Visegrad with Gyuri, and it is three weeks today that I wrote in my diary how unutterably happy I am. Why can suddenly and unpredictably everything change? Today it is raining. I put on a pullover because I feel cold. The light is on, it is dark outside at two o'clock in the afternoon in June, and inside, in me, everything feels the same. My soul feels cold; sometimes a cold shiver runs down my spine. Something is hurting me so much in there, so very much. But I did not shed a tear and I will not cry, even if I spoil my life, even if I marry someone, anyone—even if all my life I will be longing after him, I will not shed a tear. I received a short farewell letter from Gyuri. This is what he wrote:

"For the sake of the ideal, pure memories, do not ask anything. Do not attack me with my own words, because they were always true. I am weak; to lie, to play, and...to believe. I am ending it. We will not meet, do not call me by telephone and do not write to me. — If you can, I beg you to forgive me. Gyuri"

BUDAPEST, 1943. JUNE 5

There is no happiness on this earth, only a pleasant or unpleasant life. Well, my life will be pleasant. I will not fight for him; there is no sense in that. If he himself does not want me…if he does not need me… Today I grew much older again. There was only one man I believed in, who I did not think would lie to me, whom I trusted, to whom I would have entrusted my whole life. Now I will not even have that one man. Actually everything is so simple. Stella with her weakness was stronger. Since I am more proud than to show my weakness, I lost him. I am not angry at Stella—I wish her to be completely happy because I am no longer there between the two of them. And now I finally learned that one thing is not permitted: to be sincere, because in that case this is the end. One must lie and play and cheat, lead everyone by their nose and then laugh behind their back. Use everyone, be selfish to the extreme, take all and give none. And never be in love—do not love anyone. Be well dressed, attractive, promise everything, and remain cool; this is needed to gain victory, to conquer, to succeed. And my heart should be buried, trampled deep into the earth, so that no one ever would be able to find it.

However, the month of May was beautiful, real, blooming, fragrant, colorful, musical, warm May. The nicest May in my life.

1943. JUNE 14, MONDAY

It is one week today that I received the letter from Gyuri. Oh God, it feels as if a whole year had passed since then. A mournful year, full of pain, bitterness, disappointment, tears, and sorrow. Because I cried. I cried when the priest spoke in church about the immeasurable, dark, bottomless loneliness, which we feel in its entirety when we see that our fellow-men do not care for us and in which only the closeness of God provides solace. This is when I became fully aware how much richer Stella is compared to me. She is never alone because she has her faith, which fulfills her entire life and gives her strength to suffer. And then she has Gyuri next to her, who helps her forget her worries and troubles and bridges any difficulties. I will be lonely forever in this life from now on. I cannot be happy anymore; at most I can have an eventful life. One week ago…how much has changed in one week? I would like to travel, to be far from here where I have so many memories with him, like today when I was strolling on the Rozsa Hill, where so many times we took long walks together, talking quietly or just lost in thought, sensing each other's presence and not even wishing for anything more. I remember Tary Ila, the fortune teller, as if she had been right; was this then the great love affair that I was waiting for so much and that she predicted will end quite unexpectedly and very suddenly? Alas, it was short lived, not enough nourishment to last a lifetime. Truly, I still cannot imagine that he would never return to me again. I am still expecting his letter, his phone call, or that he simply would drop in on such a rainy afternoon like today. And then the clouds would part and the sky would clear, the heat of the summer sun would shine again and illuminate the whole world!

1943. JULY 21, WEDNESDAY

What is it I want to write? I don't even know. Nothing much happened this summer so far. Now I am in Ungvar. I came here for a short holiday. The July sun is sweltering. I am visiting with Zsuzska and Gabi, my cousins, whom I usually met in Kassa with the rest of the family during our school vacations.

Ungvar is a nice city, smaller than Miskolc but perhaps nicer; there is a beautiful walk along the Ung river, the Galago, with benches and flowers bordering the river. That is where we met all the young people, Zsuzska's friends. They are about 20, 21 years old. Here I met Szilagyi; he is a very witty, intelligent, cultured boy, and I enjoy his company. I also went to Nevicke for a day with Tibor; he is romantic, sentimental, and fun to be with. They are all very likable, pleasant company. I met a lot of new people, young, first-class brains, different dispositions, different temperaments, and different characters. Here I warmed up to Gabi. She is a sweet little girl, very friendly and affectionate. She will be soon 16 years old. How I was waiting to be 16 and how nice that year was! But it passed, alas, it passed long ago.

Now I am ready to pack. Time is passing fast; it was pleasant, it was enjoyable, and it was enough. I am going to Miskolc from here.

1943. AUGUST 5, THURSDAY

I was interrupted; I had to get ready to leave. I had not been back in Miskolc since we moved to Buda, and I did not even long to go there. But now I am glad to see my city again; I am Curious how I will find, as an outsider the city, the people, the youth when long ago I was one of them. How will they receive me? With affection? Or coolly with envy? Here everyone I met talked me into studying further, to go to University. I should not become dull and uninteresting through marriage like the other girls; I should get a diploma, a doctorate. I should have a goal and strive for it. I should not give up the fight even before I begin. How nice it would be if indeed I would have meaningful work, if I had a full life, if I would not have to lean on a man. I could go abroad and live independent and free.

A lot of things happened during my stay here. Mussolini and Ciano resigned, the British occupied Sicily, and the Germans are retreating from Russia. Even here the atmosphere changed toward the Jews. People feel peace and order, thinking of men who will come home and marriages that will take place. If only it were true and peace would be here. Peace, Peace, Peace!

1943. August 12, Thursday

I am traveling back to Budapest tomorrow. I was here in Miskolc for one week. They welcomed me with affection. It is nice to come back when everybody waits for you, smiling and with open arms. Yet I did not feel as well here as in Ungvar. This is a nasty anti-Semitic place where even the official orders are overdone. They remind me that they took my father to Sianki, that they had him resign from his position as the director in the biggest trust company in Miskolc, that they threw us out of our home, the likes of which we will never have again in our life. I hate them and I hate the city. I'm rummaging among my memories as I am roaming the streets, but it does not feel good to remember. It brings me no enjoyment. I am glad to leave, and I don't wish to return soon.

What hurts me most is that Julie cooled toward me. She does not tell me things about herself as she used to; she changed a lot, and she doesn't open up to me anymore. I wonder why, what is the reason for this change. I wrote to her, but she did not even answer. I sense that she does not need me anymore; she doesn't miss me, and she doesn't want me. I invite her to Budapest, yet she does not want to come. She probably has someone who holds her here, but she will not talk about it. A while ago we were really good friends. Or the underlying reason in fact is that we are Jewish and thereby in a very unstable situation, and she does not want to take a chance to be too closely attached to us. What a pity.

Now I have no one left. The only schoolmate is Bleci with whom I kept up our friendship, now better than before. Maybe she will come up to Budapest. It would be good if she lived with us, and I would not be so lonely. She is also an only child like I am. Financially we would also need someone to live with us to contribute to the expenses. From this pension and what the prices are today, one cannot manage. I would like to work in earnest, starting in September and make at least enough money so that I would not cause my parents any financial worries. If everything would succeed the way I imagine it! Unfortunately the plan to open an English nursery is not possible right now. One cannot get a room in all of Budapest. I want to have a few students, nothing more.

Tomorrow I will be in Buda. I am a bit afraid to go up, but work will start again. And I would like to enter this year a bit differently, to be more serious. I want to study, not just have a good time. Of course I want to go to concerts, frequent the English Club, read a lot of serious books, and play the piano. It would be good if someone could help me because alone I don't have enough willpower and strength to continue. If an ambitious girl lived with us that would help me a lot. We would stimulate each other, compete with each other, and that way we could accomplish something. I would also like to take the English State Exam.

1943. SEPTEMBER 12, SUNDAY

I handed in my application to the University for the Medical Faculty, but they refused it. Tamas got all his papers and will go to Switzerland in two weeks.

There is complete disorder in Italy. The Italians ceased combat against the British and took up arms against the Germans. Who knows what will happen to us? Which side will we choose? Will we be bombed? And who will be bombing us? Perhaps the war is nearing its end. The atmosphere is uneasy. Most of the people are optimistic; only my father is pessimistic, and he informs us only of bad news. Perhap they will be fed up with the carnage, and there will be peace again. If only the 21 year olds would not have to go to the labor camps.

1943. NOVEMBER 24, WEDNESDAY

This afternoon is an exception. I am free and I am alone, so now I can catch up on my correspondence. I am listening to wonderful jazz music coming from London, and at times like this my little booklet turns up. I learned that Gyuri joined up, but I have no news where they went. I am working a lot; I have thirteen students, and this month I earned 404 pengo. It is true that I spent five hundred. I buy my own dresses, and I get only my room and board from home. This is a very good feeling because I am accepted by my parents—they take me more seriously since I became a breadwinner. True, I will be 20 years old in two months. My God how time flies. M. Agi became a bride; she will make a good match, and they will move to Budapest. I hope this will bring us closer together, and we will be good friends again. Slowly everybody gets married around me, and now I can also imagine that I would find a husband.

I would find a sweet little apartment, which I could keep nice and tidy, and a youthful, understanding husband who is my best friend, my pal, my love... Who knows if this will come true and when?

Before marriage I would like to go abroad to learn and gain experience. I have great demands and regrettably circumstances are unfavorable. War weddings? Unfortunately I have seen enough of them. This is not the time for planning. We can live only for the present, and the present offers almost nothing. How I yearn for the end of the war and hope for peace, a tranquil life, independence, and freedom. This is why I would like to go abroad to get a taste of that too. Of course to reach this, it is essential that the war would end. I am curious to know, if Tamas will get to Switzerland, or will he too be compelled to bide his time till the end of the war?

1944. MAY 28 SUNDAY, AT DAWN

I am sitting here next to the radio. I am on duty. I was reading what I wrote up to now, and I will wind up and answer every question. Since Gyuri joined his unit, I have heard nothing about him. He wrote a letter to me, in which he said how sorry he is for what he did, that he was insane and he now sees that I am the only one who counts and gives meaning to his life. I answered to the address he gave, but I think he will never receive it; they are moving them on toward the Russian front.

Tamas remained in Budapest. Francis, in a letter, asked me to marry him under these extraordinary circumstances. I wrote to him and nicely said that I will not marry now—neither him nor anyone else. His answer to that was a farewell forever. Who knows where will they take him? Everything came crashing down—the hopes, desires, plans, dreams, the house of cards, the love affairs, work, and the future. Nothing remains, not even the Tomorrow. Here is the moment, which is still in my hand, and then it slips away too, and we don't know what the next moment will bring. Much...I could write an awful lot, but it's not worth it. If...if? This "if" is life. I wish I could continue here, where I left off.

1944. NOVEMBER 20, MONDAY

I have a sudden fancy for writing. These cold winter evenings are so long that one does not know how to kill the time. I am not in the mood now either to read or to sew, so I am writing. It is already November, and I am still alive. The hardest part is still ahead of me. I wonder if we will escape this unharmed. And how? Can we survive this holocaust? I cannot even look toward the distant future now. I am not interested to know what will be "afterward." Only what will be tomorrow? And in the morning when I wake up? The days go by with...nothing. Life has absolutely no meaning. It is the war that gives meaning and value to life. A person's life is such a miserable, petty affair. And how much we are attached to it! How we clutch at straws. Still, I want to live. Perhaps because so far I lived so little? Perhaps because I think only henceforth will I be able to enjoy life's beauty? After all, I only saw its ugly side day after day.

I became disillusioned slowly from everything, especially from love, which does not exist, or at least not now in these stormy times. Mainly I am disillusioned in men, all men. I hate them and I want to hate them forever. Because they are all the same; they all want the same thing, only their means are different. One is better mannered; the other is more common, or perhaps only more candid. They are infinitely selfish, and compared to them I am not selfish enough, not cunning enough. But I will be. You will see, Magda, that I will succeed, because I want to. So far I succeeded in everything I wanted very much. I do want to survive this war. If only I would succeed in this too. I am thinking a lot about my past like an old woman, reflecting on this twentieth year of mine like the previous ones. Time is flying, and where are all my great dreams, my great desires, my great plans, my great expectations, which were all slowly born from complete modesty? Where are they now from being realized? And the bleaker my present, the more I demand from my future.

The future…if I reach it, if I live to see it. And Gyuri, will you return and help me reach my goals? Won't you? Do you hear me? Will you answer my call?

CHAPTER III

1945. PEACE IS HERE!!!!

MAY 25, FRIDAY

Finally an end to the war: the massacre, the gunfire. The bombs are not dropping anymore, the machine guns are quiet, and the arrow-cross men are not patrolling the city with their armbands on their arms and their guns on their shoulders. Peace is here! Gone is the mortal danger, and we survived this holocaust, the persecution of the Jews, this pogrom and two months of the siege of Budapest. Now we are approaching a better, nicer life, and with every day, every hour, every minute we are getting further away from evil and closer to a peaceful future. PEACE! It arrived, it is here, palpable and surrounding me, but alas, not in me. Somehow I do not feel at peace, and I cannot enjoy it. I am still very much under the influence of what has happened. The recent past is weighing heavily on me. It is still almost my present; there is no distance yet where to observe it from. Everything still hurts. My father is not yet home, and there is no inner peace for me; I am still living the war.

And now I will attempt to describe what happened up to now, what we survived, what we went through. Now that I can write in the past tense, now that I don't have to fear that my diary will give me away, for which I could have paid with my life, and while I am still here in Budapest and all is still fresh in my mind.

I will start before the 19th of March, 1944, when I was sick for two months. I lost a lot of weight, and became debilitated. I got thirty injections and daily I had to lie down for three hours in front of the open window under my eiderdown cover. Three hours every day! How terrible that was. My thoughts were chasing each other, and I tortured myself, suffered inhumanly. The doctor suspected my lungs. I was reading *The Magic Mountain* by Thomas Mann, and I imagined myself in a sanatorium on a high mountain surrounded by coughing sick people, lying in the sun on a terrace from morning till noon and from noon till the evening, philosophizing over the transitory nature of mankind. I thought life already had come to an end for me. I would not become a woman, would not be able to have children, no man would look at me, and all the pleasures of life would cease for me forever. Could I have had tuberculosis? Fortunately it was only a nightmare!

On Sunday, March 19, when I could get up, my rest-cure finally came to an end, and I finished the injections. It was the very first Sunday when I wanted to go out to see people. I wanted to continue where I left off before my illness, and while the others were partying and enjoying themselves. It was Tamas who burst in the door like Evil himself with the news, relating to us calmly, as if *life* would not depend on it: the Germans had entered Budapest. I did not want to believe him; simply this news could not reach my consciousness. I could not grasp what he said. The Germans are here. So what? I could still go to the English Club! I still could teach my pupils! There are still movies to see and coffee houses to meet my friends! And only slowly, with difficulty, did I wake up and understand the meaning of these words.

This is what we feared since the war broke out, since we heard what happened in Austria and Slovakia and Poland and everywhere the Germans marched in. And now they came here, and here they start their vandalism. As I finally understood this, I was convinced that I will not live more than twenty-four hours because they will pick me up, drag me away, and put me to death. And only one feeling strengthened in me minute by minute: with a shrill cry, I said, "no, no, a thousand times no!" I still want to live, since until now I haven't lived while others were enjoying their lives! I will not remain here in this "prison" where, if I wait, with every approaching moment the executioner can come for me. Away from here—anywhere!

So we got started. First we went to our family doctor, asking him to hire me in the hospital as a cleaning woman. He was not willing to do so. Mother went to the nuns and asked that if they should take me in, I would be willing to convert, but they would not take me. Nobody helped.

Meanwhile the days wore on. On the streets police cars were sounding their alarms and picking up people. The police also removed the Jews from the trams, never to return home again. Some Jews just went to buy a newspaper or make a phone call, and their families never saw them again.

I thought of Robert, one of my students. Perhaps he could help, give me advice. He was from Slovakia, and he claimed to be Aryan. He had come to me the first of February; our friends in the building had recommended that he learn English from me.

He was sensible, talented, intelligent, and sympathetic. My Aunt Szeren, mother's oldest sister, was visiting us from Kassa, and she liked him. Couldn't he be considered for a husband? (Many girls had the idea that if they were married the Germans wouldn't take them away.) But I did not even think of anything like that. Aunt Szeren also told us she knows of some acquaintances, Slovak Jews hiding here in Budapest. Hearing about this I got encouraged to ask Robert if he would be able, being also from Slovakia, to get their advice on what could be done because I couldn't just sit here and idle my time away waiting for what fate held for me. And he helped more than I expected, more conscientiously than I had hoped.

First he obtained papers for the three of us, me, my mother, and my father. They were expensive, but were excellent, authentic-looking official documents. I became Danos Maria, Roman Catholic.

False papers, 1944. I changed my identity.

With these documents he built up my strength and self-confidence. He gave me orders that I immediately had to carry out. "Rent a sublet at once and look for a job." By April one I had an apartment, a living room with a daybed in a co-op apartment that a widow owned. She had to pass through to get to her bedroom, but it had a bathroom that served as a kitchen too. The kitchen was also used by another lady, also her tenant. She was a cosmetician in the Ritz Hotel. My landlady was a nice, simple protestant woman, sufficiently naïve, just suitable for my purpose. I was not a familiar face in the area, nobody knew me since it was the other side of Buda, known as the Horthy Circle. It was a nice new section, called Ujbuda.

With this decision I also had to give up teaching English. The most important group I had was in a hospital in Kobanya, where all the young medical students felt that they needed to know English. I went there by trolley and bus, but since there were many in a group it was worthwhile for me to spend the time traveling there. Now I had to tell them that I was moving to the countryside, and I said good-bye to all of them.

Slowly I started to carry my things over to the apartment, dresses, shoes, always with one suitcase coming and going and walking confidently with my Aryan papers in my handbag. However as soon as I closed the door in my parent's home, I became small again. I knew I would not remain here for long. I had constant arguments with them. They did not dare to oppose me or talk me out of it because here it was a matter of *life*, my life, and they could not take that responsibility. But they tried to frighten me. "Others have no problem. They live quietly at home with their families, while this could be your undoing. The detectives will find you." I tried my best to convince them, and I stood by my decision. Somehow there was a sure feeling in me that I must survive this, that I couldn't perish. I still had a lot of work ahead of me in this life, and I couldn't abandon this mud-ball planet with only my twenty years of knowledge—twenty years—the first twenty years of life's experiences.

And then Dudi gave me the last nudge. On April 20 she arrived from Kassa with nothing but the dress that she had on her, together with her best friend S. Marta, exactly as they escaped from the ghetto. Slowly all the Jews were moved into a ghetto from the provinces, and from there were loaded into wagons, seventy of them into one wagon with two buckets. One had drinking water, the other served as a toilet. Her mother and father, Aunt Szeren and her husband, and all our other relatives were already in the brickyard without a roof, in the open air, soaked from the rain, cold from the wind, and not knowing for how long and what more was awaiting them. As soon as my father heard this, he uttered the decisive words. "You are right; you can go." And with those words I started off with the last of my luggage, my bedding, into the unknown, into the struggle and privation of *life*. And so my march took me into my rented room.

A few times I still went home to my parents. While there I had to sew the yellow star on my dress, so I went to the apartment of the Aldor family who lived in the same building. They helped me out. I loathed wearing it because I was humiliated by it, as if it would cry out that I was less worthy than the others. I knew inside me that I was every bit as worthy. So I went back with the star on my dress, and from my old home I slipped out in the dusk or at dawn like a thief who steals from fate because she had stolen back her parents for a few hours.

Shortly an ordinance came: I would have to report for the laborcamp. After what happened in Slovakia, we already knew what that meant. So I was declared officially missing. "She was picked up by the Gestapo," my poor mother said, getting quite sick from it. Her sisters were indeed taken by the Gestapo from Kassa by then. My dear Aunt Szeren came to us truly to say good-bye. She visited us in Budapest for the first and the last time. She was my favorite aunt; she had no children and I was her favorite niece. We received a postcard from Uncle Joska, Dudi's father, saying good-bye.

I took the number 61 trolley, and as it was rumbling, the window was open and the wind was stinging my eyes wet with tears. It was only the wind. I was not panicking and was not imagining things. I did not fantasize and so I didn't even cry. I acknowledged that this had to be. But inside something was hurting terribly. A heavy millstone pressed on my heart.

And then Dudi got married. For years Uncle Joska was friendly with a family in Budapest through business connections. Sometimes he took Dudi with him. They had a son, Frici, who liked her a lot, but she did not take this seriously. When Dudi escaped from the deportation in Kassa and came to Budapest, she stayed with Frici's family. Considering the circumstances, they all felt it would be best for them to get married. By now men were drafted one after the other, and soon Frici was called in too. I told Frici, "Don't leave Dudi here alone; go to live in hiding like me." But I talked to them in vain; Frici joined the army (in a labor camp), and by the time I could get false papers for Dudi, a detective from Kassa recognized her on the street, took her back with him, and from there of course it was onward with the others, and she was deported by the Nazis.

My life was simple but with some excitement. The first was my registration, which the police department never saw. (I showed my false papers to the building commandant.) Everyone had to be registered at the police when changing their residence. The second bit of excitement was with the food stamps, which arrived by mail to everybody, issued by the government. I explained that I got those at my aunt's. (My "aunt" was my mother). Actually my mother sometimes gave me homemade pastry that she baked when we met, in the beginning at the Aldor's, later at Uncle Bela's, and then in the store of the Feher couple. When my landlady saw the pastry, I had to explain to her that I got it from my aunt. Once she even commented, "How lucky you are that you have here such a good aunt as if she were your mother." "Well indeed," I said, "this is why my mother entrusted me to her without any worry."

I met Tamas a few times; I obtained papers for his sisters, of course through Robert. Then he joined the military and I did not hear anything further about him. I did not disclose my address to anyone; even Robert did not know it. I lived totally cut off from my old world, while I did not have a new one. When I was still at home, I organized a farewell party. I invited M. Lilli, Bleci and P. Gyorgy, and in back of my mind I said good-bye to them. Who knows if I would ever see them again. But of my plan, which was already realized, I did not say anything to any of them. I cut the last thread that connected me to my past—I started a new life, which was extremely bleak.

I put an ad in the newspaper, and I got a temporary job taking care of a two-year-old girl. Her father worked as the head of the post office, and her mother was a teacher in the gimnazium. She had a twelve-year-old brother who was a Jew hater, as he was taught and trained in school. Sometimes he even quarreled with his father who was "only" a hardened prewar anti-Semite. I liked their daughter, she could not help that she was born into such circumstances. If her brother did not spoil her, she would be a charming little girl, with nice, fine features, and if she got the proper education, perhaps she could become a talented pianist. I say that because of what she displayed: she sat down to the piano and with her tiny fingers kept hitting the keys, not with one finger but nicely with all ten as she saw her brother and her mother playing.

The child was dressed practically in proletarian clothes, untidy and dirty. Her little dresses were too long, and whatever they put on her had no chic. Since we lived in a world where air raids were a daily event, and we often went into the basement, they put the child to bed at night the way she was dressed during the day. Slowly I introduced the habit that I washed her down every morning with cold water, quickly rubbed her dry, and dressed her. Her mother and grandmother often came to see what I was doing. At least this way I got some practice to be able to get another job, because I knew I would not stay here long.

The boy was ill-bred and very nasty. Once while I was lounging around in the garden with the little girl, he came out and started to play with a small worm. "Don't think you will die so easy; first I will torture you a bit," he said and then he cut the worm into pieces while enjoying its writhing. I was thinking of the poor Jews who got into the hands of such sadistic henchmen, and cold sweat was running down my spine.

Next morning I had to take care of the girl in a hurry to clean the bedroom. When I was finished, they pushed a lot of stuff into my hands to sew, to darn, and to mend, and I was sitting and sewing till five in the afternoon. I have never seen so many torn, shabby clothes anywhere in my life. (True that so far I had not seen much at all in my life or from life in general.) I received a sixty pengo monthly salary, and I did not have a day off, including Sundays. The food was bad. Bad? I was used to better at home. The only good thing was that I could serve myself; they did not dish it out, and even if it didn't taste good I ate it because I never knew when would I get into a situation of not having any food at all.

The mistress of the house seldom played the piano, and finally once I asked her to play for me. It was a Sunday afternoon when I could have left earlier, but where would I go? I could not go to my parents, and Robert went to a "competition" as he always said when he had other plans. It was an excellent excuse, like with "business meetings" for the husbands. I never checked on him. I always tried my best to believe everything he told me, and it was easy at the beginning. Sometimes he waited for me at five o'clock, and then we went to eat dinner at the Ketter restaurant or to a movie. When I returned home at night my room was empty. I could only talk to my landlady to whom I was bragging about my boyfriend, the bank employee, who could perhaps even get serious. After this she was always waiting for me to give her an account of some new developments. She was trying to educate me and give me advice. She was lonely too, and I brought a little excitement into her life.

To get back to the piano on my job, my employer sat down to play. She started with the "Minuette" by Paderewski and continued with "Dreams of Love" by Liszt, and listening to her I could hardly hold myself back from crying. These were the same pieces I used to play some time ago. I never missed the piano as much as now when it was here before me, and I could not even hit one key lest I would give myself away that I knew how to play the piano too. Once the boy asked me the notes on the keyboard, trying to show off his knowledge. "Do you know what this is?" "C," I answered modestly. "And this?" "D" "And this?" "E". "This?" "F" "And do you know this one?" He showed me the black key. "No, what is that? "I answered and blushed for acting ignorant.

This time I met my parents at my father's friend, Bela's. One day they told us that F Jutka, my classmate from Miskolc, got married. Her husband helped her parents escape to Budapest, and they were all leaving for Palestine. That was the only transport that left Hungary. To leave Hungary meant to leave life. But staying here meant death.

Before I became a Christian nanny, my parents were contemplating marriage for me. Now more than ever a new wave of rumors were sweeping over Hungary. The girls were hoping that if they got married the same thing will happen here as in Slovakia, where the married women were not deported, only the young girls. Six of my classmates got married to boys about their own age, the ones we used to walk with on the Korzo but never considered seriously. Somehow I knew and sensed that such steps were ineffective and useless.

The next rumor among Jews was that they would be safe if they converted to Christianity; they paid heavy sums to the Church to receive the documents, but this did not help either. The Germans are more thorough, more efficient. Even if the parents had already converted years ago, their children were still counted to be Jewish. Only two grandparents were acceptable mitigating circumstances. The third rumor going around was to obtain a letter of "safe conduct," but this happened later, so I will get back to it.

The family who I worked for was planning to go to a vineyard, and they asked me to go with them for the summer. I don't know what was keeping me back more, the total isolation there and fear of all that sewing or leaving my parents, or Robert, who was the only person helping me with every problem that turned up almost daily with the authorities. I did not feel like going with them, so I put an ad in the classified again. I received only one answer, to go to the ticket office of the opera house.

I was received by a lovely young woman who immediately gained my approval (how wrong can a first impression be?), and we came to an agreement; I would receive 180 pengo and complete board, from nine in the morning till seven in the evening, with one full day off, but not Sunday. She had one child, a little girl whom I would take care of. With this position I had moved at least four rungs up the ladder. With this job I arrived into the milieu of the middle class, that which my family also belonged to, more or less.

This was in June. I went to work in the morning on the trolley and then walked up the Rozsa Hill to a nice small villa with a neglected garden. I could spend a lot of time outside with the little girl. It was good that I did not have to take her for a walk. At least I did not have to be afraid of meeting people who could recognize me. The grandmother, a divorced woman, lived downstairs on the ground floor, and it was her daughter who moved in with her together with her husband, a doctor of law. On the top floor lived a Jewish couple with their spinster daughter. They were living previously in the houses with the yellow star. The mistress of the house was very nervous, because she wanted to move up there, so I tried to comfort her. "Rest assured, madam, it is only a question of a few days and the posters will be out. They will have to move."

The Jewish woman lamented over every trifle, and they vacillated as they could not decide about exchanging their apartment for another because of an oven. By then my mistress lost her cool; she was walking up and down like a tiger, cursing as her eyes flashing with anger, and with clenched fists she screamed, "If they don't move I will have the Gestapo put them out of here!"

I knew what this meant and my heart sank, not knowing what I should do to warn these poor, ignorant Jews whose life could depend on an oven. When I found an opportunity, I went upstairs and while first talking to them about other things, I casually asked them with a blasé face, as if I were talking about the weather, when will they move? Well, they didn't know yet, and they complained that there was only one stove in that apartment where they could move to, and the stove has no oven. Suddenly I lost my temper, and I declared in an obnoxious voice, "You people will not be baking there anyway. Does moving out of here depend on this?" They looked at me as if I was their greatest enemy and a real anti-Semite , and I got their answer. "Maria, if we would be thinking like you, we would lie into a coffin here and now!" The tone was polite and reserved from then on between us—they were afraid of me.

By the end of June my parents had to move into the marked houses with the yellow star of the ghetto. I was barely alive from all the anxiety because I thought that after that the deportation would begin. Mother and father got a room in the apartment of P. George's parents; they carried only their most needed belongings: the twin sofa, a wardrobe, and a trunk. Everything else remained in our apartment on Bajvivo street. We had many wooden crates down in the basement, including all my valuable trousseau my mother had prepared for me through the years for when I would get married. (She thought it was safe there together with many other crates of the other residents in the building.) I was convinced that either here or there everything would perish anyway. I was most surprised, but at the same time it made me deathly nervous, at the optimism of these Jews, their pettiness, that they still could not comprehend and adapt to their present situation.

The child I took care of was a two-year-old little girl. The moment I met her I found her unpleasant. She was a typical Aryan child, whining, spoiled, badly brought up. She had a strong lisp, and I could hardly understand her. Kata.

Kata, the little girl I took care of, 1944.

92

It was interesting to observe the game chance played on me. When I was looking for my first job, I saw an ad in this same street, and I came here with Robert on a beautiful bright sunny Sunday morning. I was told that the job was filled. Now, after five weeks this job was still open, or perhaps the person was not acceptable, so they hired me. "As it was written."

When the Jews had to move, Robert moved also. He was very clever the way he managed it. He rented a very nice studio apartment and a friend of his, W. Sari, moved all her furniture into that place instead of the one in the ghetto. This way Robert got a well-furnished home without having to spend any money on it. When I finished my day on the job, I went there and put things in order and put away his belongings. At times like this he was not home; he was on the field training. I also gave him many things, trifles and all that he asked for and needed. This was the least I could do for him after how much he helped me in these difficult times. He also stored a suitcase for us in the basement with my father's clothing in case something happened and he had to flee, here he would be able to change.

In the evening when I returned home it was only my empty room that awaited me and the two old gossipy women. I always had to tell my story. Many times I was glad that I could talk about the little girl, the maid, the doctor, and his wife because this distracted attention from myself, and I would not be always preoccupied with myself. Everything was permitted but contemplation, because thinking would drive me crazy. How could I possibly live with the tremendous pain about our relatives who were deported in Slovakia—seventy members of my mother's family—and to be in constant agony and fear for my parents and my own solitary life, which was difficult to get used to? I was hanging in space like a piece of land ready to brake off the earth. Still only one thread held me here: the will to live. Usually once a week I met my parents. It was mainly my mother who bothered me with her constant dread, anxiety, inhibitions, and pettiness so that somehow or other she succeeded to make me lose my zest for life completely. Again it was Robert who shook me up, did just the opposite from my parents. He was always positive and full of optimism.

By this time my dad also rented an apartment so that if suddenly anything would happen, he would have a place to go. He did this with great difficulty upon my express wish and forcefulness so I would leave him in peace, not from his own conviction. He used his false papers and told the landlord that he came to Budapest on business from Debrecen quite often, which was why he needed the apartment.

Time was moving slowly; it was only the end of June. Robert's attitude changed toward me since he felt I didn't need him anymore, that I could stand on my own two feet now. I missed him a lot because he was the only person I could talk to sincerely, to whom I did not have to lie. He knew who I was, and he could always cheer me up with his blessed good humor. I think that he was a carefree, happy-go-lucky person who loved to live and was chasing life.

Last May, when the Jews had to put the yellow star on (I was Christian, so it did not concern me except when I visited my parents' apartment), Robert and I took a walk in Taban, where we enjoyed the beautiful green grass, the sun, and the spurge flowers that peeked out joyfully with their yellow heads between the grass. "How many Jews?" said Robert, reflecting quietly. Yet he never revealed to me that he was one too.

Once we had dinner in the Ketter when he pointed out a young man to me in the next booth. "This is my friend. I already talked to you about him; he is the one who shares my apartment." I recognized him immediately—he was R. Pali. Dudi had introduced him to me when we had dinner at the Tarjan. I did not say anything to Robert, only that he looked very familiar to me. Dudi was still here then. I went to see her and described this young man to her and also whatever I knew from Robert about him. Everything clicked. They are both from Zsolna. The next time we met I asked him, "Robert, tell me, is it possible that two people from Zsolna should not know each other? It is a small town." "No," he answered. "But this friend of yours is R. Pali from Zsolna! I know him." "No you are mistaken; he is an Aryan." And he told me a name. This total distrust hurt me immensely. He knew all about me yet he made a fool of me? Weeks later, when he had a card party in his place and I went up there, Pali was there too, and I talked to him. He also recognized me and immediately asked about Dudi. By that time the poor girl was already taken away back to Kassa.

I lived two different lives. One was like this, when I took part at a card party to kibitz four boys by turns. I drank liqueur and listened to the radio. I was a Jewess in hiding, and I was again a bit D. Magda. And my other life, when during my work the maid pestered me, did not give me proper food, and the child misbehaved. Here I was a self-respecting Christian yet more underprivileged than ten Jews. It is interesting how one lifestyle influenced the other. I felt that the young men did not show as much interest in me as in those days when my parents were around and my home and my possible dowry were behind me. I became an average girl, having absolutely nothing and even an uncertain life. People did not think as highly of me as before.

Now I am sorry that I could not write in my diary at that time because I should have preserved those countless thoughts that were then in my mind. During July and August life was moving on with little action. The only change was that in the villa a new maid was hired, which turned out to be very good for me because this woman flattered me and stuffed me like a goose. And I was eating because I thought again that I did not know when a time would come that I would not have anything to eat. At least I should have some reserve.

At this time we experienced heavy English bombing. They did not bomb this district of Buda, the Rozsa Domb, which had all the residential villas. The doctor and I were watching how the bombs were dropping; the planes were rumbling and after them everything burst into flames, and clouds of black smoke rose toward the sky. I actually enjoyed it, and I wished that they would destroy as much as possible of this city, which did not deserve anything other than death and devastation.

The mother and grandmother with the child were downstairs in the laundry room trembling. I did not wish anything better for them. "This is the time they should chase the Jews out to the streets so they would be gunned down," said the mistress once, and I could not say a word. Each time after the sound of the air-raid alarm stopped, I telephoned my mother to see if they were alive and whether there was some trouble where they were living. So far they were all right.

Sometimes Robert phoned me and someone from the family picked up the receiver. They noticed that he spoke with a

German accent. They asked me if my boyfriend was a German officer. I said yes. I learned this also from Robert, that people have such a vast imagination they always ask questions, and we only have to agree with them. The doctor even asked me, "Doesn't he have on his sleeve such a...I did not know what he was explaining to me, but I answered as quickly as a flash, "Yes he has." From then on my boyfriend was a Gestapo officer. And this stuck with me so much so that when in September it got difficult to obtain provisions, the doctor raised the thought that they should go to the countryside by car and that way bring back a lot of food. "Best would be a military auto, which would not be searched. But since here is Maria's Gestapo officer, he could obtain a car! They can travel down together, and we will have all we need to eat." "I'm sorry sir, you are late. We broke up already," I said. (Boy I got out of this one!)

Actually it was quite pleasant to be in the villa. I often dressed in shorts and T-shirts. When Kata was sleeping I would bask in the sun or read. They had a nice library, and I received books from them. They had fruit trees in the garden, and I picked the fruit and ate as much as I wanted. Only once I had a small clash with the grandmother. The doctor was picking cherries from one of the cherry trees, and I was helping him when she called out from her window. "Peter dear, do not pick all of them off; leave some for the Bessy's when they arrive." (This was her other daughter, the actress from Kolozsvar, who was about to go to the Balaton and en route stopped over with her husband in Budapest.) Peter phlegmatically answered OK and kept on picking the delicious crunchy fruit. I did too. Soon the old woman called to me in an irritated voice. "Maria, I already said that you should not pick the fruit from the tree. There will be none left for my daughter, and you already ate enough."

Without a word I came down from the tree and did not look toward her anymore. When her dear daughter arrived, not once did it occur to her to go near the tree to pick the cherries, and the fruit was either rotting on the tree or the thrush ate it since we did not touch it anymore.

Bessy the actress, together with her husband, knew how to curse the Jews. I was just listening to the rightist comments one after the other as she told about what good terms they are on with the German officers, they visit their homes, etc. Of course this all counted as bragging. She also wanted to show off that she was learning English, and she said, "She go to town." It was on the tip of my tongue to correct her ("she goes to town"), when at the last second I stopped myself. I could not show that I knew English; it would give me away. That would be tragic. She also said among other things, "We already live in a nice clean city, but you are still in this dirty, smelly Pest, which is full of Jews." That is to say from Kolozsvar (where they lived, another town that changed hands between Hungary and Rumania), where everybody was already deported. And they did not have so much humanity as to feel pity for these poor people who used to be their neighbors and now were robbed of all their belongings, bankrupted financially, and with their nerves shattered when they were loaded into wagons and then finished off. Would you think they could have felt sorry for them because they no longer needed to envy them? No, they rejoiced over their misery. They rejoiced because now they lived better than ever before, enjoying their prosperity since there was no more competition.

One morning my mistress received me with the news that Sunday they were going to Leanyfalu to visit some friends of theirs with the boat on the Danube, and they are also taking Kata, so I had to go with them too. My first thought was that there was always an identity check on a boat, and also there would be many people on board and that I might meet some acquaintances. I instinctively wanted to decline, but then I thought it over and decided to ask Robert first. I called him and asked that he come to meet me right away. I must talk to him over a very important matter. In the afternoon while Kata was sleeping, I met him outside and I told him what this was all about. He scolded me. "Why wouldn't you go? First of all you would take part in a bit of recreation and second, when finally once you have to use your papers, you do 'you know what' in your pants. At least you get through your first test." I listened to him and I went, although this was not so simple. After all my skin was at stake—it was my life that was in danger.

We had a beautiful day. The child was so sweet, and everyone was raving about her, taking photos of her and many thought that I was her mother. This almost felt good. The couple who invited us was very pleasant and accepted me as one of them, as their equal. They offered me food and delicious coffee liqueur, we joked, and at the bridge table they invited me to kibitz. The man was an auditor; they were very well off. The trip on the way back was also very nice on the ship. I enjoyed the breeze, which tasseled my hair; I delighted in the towering waves surrounding the ship; and I contemplated about the whole day, which somehow resembled a little of my former life.

I got through the identity check without any difficulty. I presented my police ID, which had my photo (this is what Robert had made for me at the earliest time) with a confident big smile. They saluted and thanked me. A big stone fell off my heart, for now I knew that my papers are good and I didn't have to be afraid anymore.

Slowly the political climate was getting better. The Jews were living quite well in the yellow-star houses; they were free to move around and even removed the star when they went out on the streets. My dear father also met me like that in one or another small street, covering the star, and he brought me some beigli made with poppy seed or some other pastry that my mother baked, although I really did not need it. I had excellent food at my job, the family members were all big eaters, and I ate the least among them but still much more than before in my old home. I put on weight, but I did not mind it.

By now it was the middle of July. The *front* was nearing; the Russians were not far from the Karpat Mountains, which circled Hungary, and the Jews thought that they will smoothly escape the war unharmed. Now the Christians started to be scared. The other day my mistress said, "What should we do if the Russians come? Shall we obtain Jewish papers?" Her face lit up as someone who had a terrific idea. "How come?" I asked with an ignorant face. "Well the same as the Jews now obtain Christian papers, and they are hiding with them." "You can't be serious!" I exclaimed indignantly. "Are these Jews such vile scoundrels?" (She cursed the Jews so often; I also had to do the same.) "Well don't you know that?" she said surprised. And then getting back to the same subject, she remarked, "Anyway others already thought that I was Jewish!" "Me too," said the maid who came in to set the table and overheard this discussion. "Nobody ever took me for a Jew," I said with an innocent face, but inside I almost burst from laughter.

The mother of Kata was a young and pretty socialite, but she did not know much about housekeeping or about the practical side of life. When she hired me she never asked any information about me, although I told her that she could inquire at my previous post even by telephone. She already saw on my face that she could trust me, as she said, and she ushered me into a home where every closet, every drawer was open and where I was alone all day only with the maid. She did not keep her belongings in order; perhaps she did not even know what she owned. I could have taken whatever I wanted to.

The second maid while I was working there was very decent (or only curious?), and she sorted the linens, ironed them, and put them all in order so that it looked like the picture of what a linen closet should be. One day she brought my attention to some men's shirts and handkerchiefs, which had unfamiliar monograms and were put aside on the top shelf. I made a very mysterious face, and as if one would discover a great secret, I whispered, "Surely they are from Jewish property." "Oh, miss, I did not dare to say that, though I was also thinking about it, but who could have owned them?" M.F. She invented a name and from then on referred to them always by that name. The previous maid, who was here before, still worked in the villa. She was a real tattletale and told us that the Jews gave this family a lot of things, fur coats, an electric gramophone, fine books, carpets, etc., which they were keeping in the opera house. They were stupid to do these things so openly, when there was a strict punishment for it. Then one day the maid received me with the news that she could not hold it inside her anymore and asked our mistress what kind of shirts were these with the strange monograms. "A gentleman who went broke sold them to my husband not long ago," she answered. "Poor gentleman. He must have been truly reduced to poverty if he sold even his handkerchiefs," the maid replied.

I did not meet Robert often, but one evening he and his friends had dinner at the Kis Royal restaurant, and he invited me too. We ate a big meal, coupled with champagne, and we were all in high spirits. After dinner they served cantaloupe topped with ice-cream. What a beautiful and delicious desert it was. After that we all went to Robert's apartment and sat down to a great card party, except for myself. They played for huge sums, poker, chemin—hard gambling games. I did not even like to watch them; I did not understand it and had no interest in it. The excitement of the games did not captivate me, and money did not attract me. Robert played cards a lot these days. I could not dissuade him. Generally I felt as if he had lost his inner strength. He missed his parents terribly, he was homesick, and only card games could distract him from his thoughts.

One morning while going to my job I met R Pali and asked him to talk to his friend Robert because he was not doing well lately. He misunderstood me and answered that I should let Robert go his own way. Perhaps they already talked about me and how I might be a burden to him, but he did not want to tell me. I did sense this some time ago and I mentioned it to Robert, but he avoided the answer and was beating about the bush. He said he was in the kind of mood when he casts away everything and everybody and he felt that he would lose me too. He admitted that when I will not be near him, he will miss me. At that time I could not make heads or tails out of this, but now hearing Pali I saw the situation clearly. Sunday morning when I had my day off, I stopped by his place; Pali was there too. Just then we heard the air-raid sirens. Robert went down to the basement, but I stayed in the apartment with Pali. We talked a lot, and I told him that I was not in love with Robert but I needed him because he was the only person I could turn to when I needed advice or if I got into some trouble. When the alarm was over, Robert entered and Pali departed. I asked for some odds and ends of mine that I had left with him, like our iron from my old home. I collected the knickknacks and left. This was on August 1, 1944. I never saw him again, not even by chance. So now the last thread that tied me to my past was torn.

From then on I remained a nanny. When the parents went out for the evening, I stayed at work late; I gave the child her bath; I often made her oeufs a la neige, which was her favorite; I put her to bed and prayed together with her; and then I had my supper, and on nice summer evenings I walked home alone. Home, meaning that small sublet room where really and truly I could not have any privacy because my landlady would sit down with me to chat.

One such evening the parents were away with their friends, and I stayed with Kata longer than usual. I put her to bed and sat in the next room reading a book when I heard that she was making a funny noise, like coughing or choking. I ran in, opened her mouth wide, and saw something stuck in her throat. Quick as lightning I reached in with my fingers and pulled out…a bobby pin! She almost swallowed it. We always kept a nice bow in her hair during the day, but at night I was told to just keep the bobby pin in. This is what I did, but she must have taken it out of her hair and was chewing on it when it accidentally slipped down her throat. When I realized what I had done, I almost fainted. It dawned on me what could have happened if I was not there that very moment. And even though they instructed me to keep the bobby pin in her hair for the night, they would have held me responsible.

I was darned lucky.

Sometimes on my day off I went to a movie, alone, or I visited Uncle Bela where I felt at home because they were people I liked. Sometimes I was able to meet my parents. This was my life. I was glad when it would get dark, meaning another day passed. I lived in the present and did not think of tomorrow. My life was pretty empty, and I felt empty too. I did not even have the strength to try to remember my past. It did not give me any comfort or enjoyment. There was no chance I would run into my girlfriends; I had no news from anyone.

Meanwhile the Jews lived "splendidly" in the yellow-star houses; the peasants delivered all kinds of foods from chickens to geese and all the good things that the Jews loved. They came from the villages and sold to the ghettos because the Jews paid better than the Christians. Since the Jews were not allowed to work, they were condemned to rest. They played cards, had discussions, and in some places the youth got together and were even dancing. That is why my mother was so upset with me. She felt that the Jews lived secure lives and their well-being was taken care of, and I instead was working hard in constant uncertainty, endangering my life and gave up all the beauty that life has to offer. Actually this was not true.

It seems that my mistress was satisfied with my work and one day she offered me tickets to the opera house for the entire Wagner Cycle. Of course I could not resist. I thanked her and in spite of the risk that someone might recognize me, I attended every one of them. They were fabulous performances, the scenery was exceptional, and even though the reason that they played it now was because it was Hitler's favorite, I thoroughly enjoyed it.

Also not all was gloom. I loved the sunset, the ruddy clouds, the blue of the sky as the last rays of the sun lights up the lacy edges of the clouds. Then there was Kata, who made many of my hours delightful and cheerful. In the evenings I was reading books, submerged in the imaginary world of the writers, and I would be completely relaxed. If the pain was too strong, throbbing inside me, I went to seek relief in films. Somehow I did not think that the end was nearing, like the others. I had the feeling that this would last till the end of time, and I did not have as much strength to grumble or revolt. I suffered without a word because I felt I must suffer to be able to endure to the end and stay alive. I terribly missed that I could not write. I had no friend anymore to whom I could tell everything. I had constant disputes with my parents. They were paying for the apartment my father rented, and they did not move in. According to my father, the owner found them suspicious and he could not find enough excuses why not to move in. The situation was also very calm at that moment, so much so that he wanted to give up the whole thing. I asked him to first look for another place and then he could give this one up. But I was talking in vain; he did not listen to me.

Then a new option arrived, a new rumor emerged—a letter of safe conduct. Every Jew tried to get a Swedish or Swiss "Letter of Safe Conduct" to be under the protectorate of those neutral countries. By those means they would become exempted under the laws which were passed for the Jews. They also opened up the buildings of those neutral countries and took in the Jewish refugees, mostly children under 12 and the young under 21 until they were packed to the hilt and had to refuse many more who were standing outside trying to get in.

It was true; these people did not have to wear the yellow star. My father asked me if he should apply for a letter. In my opinion whatever the Jews would do was in vain—as Jews they were always in danger for their lives and there was only one way out, not to be a Jew. However I told him in any case he should do it; it can do no harm. So he gave me instructions to have seven small photos made of me as well, which were needed to attach to the papers. In getting these pictures I made a thoughtless error. (Of course I saw that only later.) I entered an unknown photo shop and gave them the order. When I went to pick it up they asked me in the store why I needed the photos since they were exactly the size and number of copies the Jews were ordering for the letters of safe conduct. I expressed my amazement at such coincidence and that I needed something like this too. And I cleared out of the store as fast as I could. If the man was a bit malicious toward me he could have called the police (the barracks of the gendarme were in the neighborhood), and that would have been the end of me. To lose my life because of a photograph is like slipping on a banana peel! Small acts like that were exactly when people were caught and shot then and there. Never again did I dare to go near that store. I gave the pictures to my father who, together with the applications, carried them with him in his pocket and never handed them in.

There was also another new ordinance that made the situation of the Jews easier. Great artists, writers, actors, doctors, and all those people who performed a useful role in the economy and cultural life in the view of the state were to receive exceptional treatment. As soon as I read that in the newspaper (and every day I searched for new orders in the papers), I told my father right away that this was what he had to do; he had succeeded at his trust company in Budapest, which he worked for and was the director of in the affiliated company in Miskolc, and that would mean a lot. I think he did not have enough self-confidence to act, and only when much later he saw how many people did receive this exception that he then applied to the company, but by then it was too late.

In September several similar facilitating orders arrived. The government was secretly negotiating with the British, and we could immediately feel its influence. I, who for years while living at home never took a daily paper in my hand, now bought the newspaper every day, browsing through from cover to cover searching for new ordinances. I did not read about the situation on the battlefield and other political sections in detail, only the headlines. However I was always well informed about everything, especially things that were important to me. After all it is not really essential to know that the Russians advanced ten or twelve kilometers again. I will surely know as soon as they arrive here. But when will that be? By that time we may not be around...

During the war I think there were few such pessimists like I was. It is possible that I did not enjoy the pleasure to immerse myself in the radio, listening to the news from London, or looking at the map flushed from the excitement calculating— if they made this route in this much time then in X days they will reach Budapest... On the other hand it could happen that a revolution breaks out, that the Finns will desert and after them the Romanians, and after them us...then those who tuned in and laughed happily, enjoying the humorists on the British radio who imitated Hitler and ridiculed him with his own words one year ago:

"Wir werden England ausradieren." (We will erase England.)

Dear God, how premature all that was!

You can write only when there is no other work to do and when you are in the mood to write without being disturbed. Since that opportunity was unavailable at the time, only as much as I remember vividly will remain on paper—things that have not faded away by the influence of new events in my life. Perhaps it is better if you forget more and more from the war and suddenly arrive at the point to think that all that might not even have been true, only a nightmarish dream. But I don't really mean that. How could you forget the years when your life is in mortal danger, when you don't know how long it will last, and if you will make it out alive?

I left off the detailed account here at the end of the summer of 1945. Now I want to fill in some gaps in the next chapter before returning to the original diary.

CHAPTER IV

2011. MIAMI, JANUARY 17

I will take over the account at this point, when I recently picked up my diary and read about all those years, bringing back the history of my adolescent and young-adult life as well as many things that I had almost forgotten, the painful stories that hurt even now as I think back and see it again in front of my eyes. It makes me wonder how I could have endured alone the pressure of the unexpected things that happened daily, when I could not even discuss anything with anyone close to me, and I could not write in my diary. This painful past influenced all my life, even though I tried to forget in order to enjoy the years ahead that I had fought so hard to attain. I really could not forget the war years. Such traumatic times remain in your memory forever. So now I will write the part that is missing from the years of 1944 and 1945 as I remember them, writing it directly in English.

It is now seventy years since I started my diary in 1941. I was then seventeen years old, in the seventh class of the gimnazium in Miskolc, when we already felt the storm gathering around us as Hitler first annexed Austria—the Anschluss—to Germany and then marched into Czechoslovakia and continued to Poland. We were anxiously watching what would happen to us because Hungary was an ally of Germany

I left off when the atmosphere in Budapest was quite positive; the Jews felt that the war would be over soon and that they would get away unharmed. It was amazing how foolishly they were thinking. When the news trickled down that the deportation of the Jews started in Slovakia, they said, well it could happen there but not in Hungary. And when it happened in Hungary in the villages, they said, well it could happen there but not in Budapest. And then it happened.

One day a truck stopped in the courtyard of the yellow-star building where my parents were staying in Pest. They piled in all the men from the apartments, and no one knew where they were taking them. When my mother saw what had happened, she snuck out through a side door with only her handbag as if she were going shopping and came to me in Buda. I introduced her to my landlady, telling her that the Russians entered Debrecen (which was true) where my parents lived in a nice house, took away my father, and she had to flee leaving everything behind. From then on we were together in my sublet. I had to buy our food stamps on the black market, and I told my landlady that I got them at my place of work—and at my work I told them I got them at my apartment. (Normally they were sent out by mail to all residents by the government.)

I was trying to find out where they could have taken my father, so I ran to the collecting stations, risking my own life because they could have held me there too. It was all in vain; among the thousands I saw, I had no chance to find him. Earlier he

110

had given up the apartment and had not done anything about obtaining the other papers, although many Jews were able to move into the Swiss and Swedish embassies and other protected buildings because they had acquired the proper papers in time.

Sadly my father had became totally apathetic, had lost all energy, motivation, and desire to live. It was just too much for him at age fifty-four to see everything collapse in front of his eyes, losing his position in the company where they robbed him of the presidency, never going back again to his beautiful home in Miskolc, having no friends around him, living in one room, and going out only during restricted hours with a yellow star on his shirt. He really did not care what would happen to him. I remember he despairingly said, "Whatever happens to the other Jews will happen to me."

I was still working in the villa, where naturally I could not speak about any of this. The fall weather was beautiful; Kata and I spent most of the day in the garden. There was a large walnut tree there, and the walnuts were ripe now, so some men came to remove the fruit. They were hitting the branches with long sticks, and as Kata was watching them, she asked, "Why are they beating the nuts? Were they naughty?" She was so cute I had to laugh. This was the only bright moment I had in those days.

My mother stayed alone in my room, going out only when she had to buy some food. She met some of the other residents, and at once they suspected her because she had showed up here just when the Jews were rounded up. She did look Jewish, with a stereotypical nose, in complete contrast to me. According to the ordinance a "building commandant" was assigned to every building by the authorities, and now some residents went to complain to him. When I got home from work, I was told about this by my landlady, and I had to go to see him. I had not thought of this before, but by my mother coming here, she had endangered my life.

I entered his home with all the confidence I could muster. I told him that my mother was forced out of her home in Debrecen, that my father was taken away by the Russians, and now that we are under such tragic circumstances, people in this building are mean enough to accuse my mother of being Jewish?! Isn't she suffering enough? It is shameful of them to behave like this instead of helping us. I have been here for five months now; I never did harm to anyone. Why would they attack my poor mother? She doesn't deserve this. After what she has gone through, they should have offered her some help instead! We had a nice house, my father was a respected citizen, and now because of the Russians she has lost everything, all her life's savings, all her belongings. And we don't know what happened to my father. You as the commandant should stop these residents who are here, living in total comfort. They should have offered her some help and sympathy instead. I acted totally indignant, and when I turned to leave, he shook my hand and apologized. I was extremely proud of myself that I pulled this off successfully. I felt that I was a true actress playing an important role—the role to save our lives.

Politically a lot of things happened that fall. In mid-October Governor-General Horthy was sent to Germany in exile, and Szalasi took over. The Germans occupied the Royal Palace in Buda, and from then on the ArrowCross Party dominated the political scene with utter brutality. They were more vicious than the Germans, more fascist than the SS. Men with the ArrowCross armband were checking identity cards of pedestrians everywhere. As I was on the way home from work one day, I noticed a bunch of people on the corner, and it looked suspicious to me. It seemed like they were picking up people, taking them away. I quickly crossed the street to the other side to avoid them. Though I had my good papers with me, I was much more cautious now than before.

Mother and I thought it would be better to find another apartment and move out of there. Anyway it was no place for both of us to live in one room with no privacy whatsoever. We went into a few buildings at the Horthy Circle and inquired if there were any empty apartments we could rent. Actually, I went in and left mother home out of caution, learning from my recent experience. By then many Christian families had left with the retreating Germans toward Germany, and I found a nice apartment on the fifth floor, fully furnished. I could see that they had left in such a hurry that the pantry was full of all the preserves they must have stored for the winter. I looked for the building commandant and asked if we could rent it for my mother and I. We agreed to his terms and soon moved in. Luckily I still had a couple of Napoleons (gold coins) left sewn into my clothes for emergencies from the time when I moved away from my parents. This was now the real emergency, and gold was the only valuable commodity for which we got enough money to support our livelihood for a good while.

As the Russians were advancing, the bombing became more frequent. The trolley had to stop, so there was no more transportation, and I could not go to work anymore. Slowly we found ourselves with little food and few places to buy any. We ate some of the preserves, which were delicious, but that was not really satisfying. So I dared to go out into the street to look around for what I could get. As I was walking to see what

I could buy in the few stores that were still open, I heard the whistle of artillery shells and jumped quickly under a doorway. (This happened quite often, and I became an expert at detecting the sound of the whistle and where it came from.) I was able to buy some bacon, but since we could not eat that without bread, I went to the bakery, which was delivering bread to the soldier's barracks nearby, and bartered some bacon for a large loaf and then went back triumphantly to show my mother what we would have to eat for a couple of days.

There was a problem with the water too. The bombs destroyed the water pipes, so we had to go to some wells to carry the water back home. The army barracks had the closest well to us, so mother and I got some buckets and went to fill them up. We did not consider that the army barracks was also a military target. Just when we were around the well, small, single-engine Russian airplanes were circling above, flying so low that we could see them clearly, and from each wing they started to shoot machine guns. We were pinned to the ground on our stomachs, not daring to budge until they moved on and hoping to survive. We were so lucky. Slowly we carried the precious water back to our apartment.

We could not stay long upstairs there because the bombs were falling and we always had to move down to the basement in a hurry. This building had a very small and poorly finished cellar, and there were too many of us to stay there except for a very short time, so a few of us decided to use the ground floor apartment, which belonged to a woman named Bozse (a real Hungarian name from a nearby village; she also spoke with a strong local accent) and her young sister. We learned that Bozse was pregnant and she welcomed my mother, thinking that she may be of some help to her.

There were also two gentlemen who preferred to stay here. One of them played the violin beautifully, which he always brought with him. He was the commandant of this building whom I had already met when I rented the apartment. He was always elegant and courteous—a real nice person. One day the bombing lasted longer than usual, and it was hard to tell what part of the city was hit. But suddenly we felt our building shaking and heard windows breaking, and in spite of it all our commandant was playing the Paganini violin concerto. He never stopped for a minute. It was a beautiful moment at a terrible time. I still see him in front of my eyes playing while the ground trembled under my feet from the bombing.

By now the weather had turned cold and, with the broken windows, we could not stay in the apartment up on the fifth floor. The top floors were more dangerous anyway. Finally when we were there eating a fruit compote and suddenly had to run down because the air-raid alarm was howling, we decided to move down permanently. There was enough room to sleep, and there was a small stove that kept the room warm. (We brought up coal from the cellar.) I had to get washed in the bathroom with the open window, but I learned that when you have no choice, you can get used to doing anything.

My mother often went downstairs to the laundry room and met the other women who were the original residents there. They also cooked down there; they were in a better position because they had lived there and were prepared with enough food for the winter. Once mother came up bringing the potato peels that the others had discarded. She chopped them and made "hamburgers" from them; it was food and we ate it. Another time in the evening we heard that the Germans were departing and that they were slaughtering their horses because they could not take them along. Mother found out that it was not far from us, and in the dark with one of the men from our building she went to get some meat. In Buda there were many underground tunnels between buildings and under the streets, so they could go at night during curfew when people were not allowed to move out. She came back with a big piece of meat dripping with blood. I'll never forget it. She prepared it so that we had enough food for a week. The open window in the bathroom served as the refrigerator. This was the first time that we ate horsemeat.

We were all excited when Bozse, the pregnant woman, went into labor. It was December, and no way could she get to a hospital. My mother cleared out the room, sent off the men, and kept only me and Bozse's sister around. Mother boiled water and helped to bring the baby into this world. I had to sterilize the scissors on the fire to cut the umbilical cord, and then I washed the baby. She was a beautiful girl, and I was really happy that I could help. What an experience! I guess it helped me that a couple of years earlier I had seen a Caesarian in the hospital in Miskolc. Although everything went quite smoothly with the birth, Bozse still had pain, and my mother knew that she had to get rid of the placenta. We had to get a doctor. So we called to the building residents to see if someone could reach a doctor living nearby and bring him over. Luckily within the hour a doctor showed up and helped to finish the delivery. He complimented me for taking care of the baby so well. From then on I had a full-time job taking care of the infant. Everyone was happy, and we soon celebrated the Christmas holiday with a bottle of wine that someone brought down to us from the building.

And slowly the New Year arrived... Budapest was encircled by the Russians, the bombing was constant, the siege of Buda had commenced, and we heard that the Germans planned to blow up the bridges on the Danube to stop the Russian army crossing over from Pest. How idiotic! Just to gain a few days, they would do such damage to a city, to ruin the most famous structures that were needed for the flow of life between Buda and Pest! Especially the Chain Bridge, which was built in 1849, the first suspension bridge built in England by William Clark and assembled on the Danube here. It has two lions on either end and, according to a folk story, when they opened it a boy pointed at the lions and laughed, "Their tongue is missing!" The engineer was so hurt by this that he jumped into the Danube and committed suicide. This bridge is the pride and joy of not only Budapest but of the whole country.

As the Russians slowly advanced, perhaps in desperation the Arrow-Cross men became even more brutal—all the Jews were deported from the yellow-star houses and the few who tried to hide were in mortal danger. Just at this time when my mother was mingling with the others in the laundry room, the son of one of the women came home and saw her there. He wore the Uniform of the Skull and Crossbones Legion and reported to the ArrowCross men that there are some Jewish women hiding here. The next day one of them with the armband came with a gun on his shoulder and ordered us to follow him. Quickly we put on coats—it was January 13, icy weather—and we walked to the headquarters with him, crossing the Horthy Circle to a small building with iron gates. We were ushered into a dark room in the basement with candles burning. There was no electricity. En route I whispered to mother:

"DENY, DENY."

They kept us there for what seemed to be hours, standing against the wall, questioning us relentlessly: Where were we from? Were we Jewish? What were we doing in that building? Why were we there? And on and on. But we denied to the bitter end that we had anything to do with the Jews and that we were Jewish.

Finally they let us go, and when we were exiting the iron gates, two guards opened it for us and one said to the other with disappointment, "We thought there will be an execution!"

Slowly we walked back to our building in the dark, physically and mentally exhausted and barely realizing that we had survived. Perhaps these murderers thought that it was senseless to kill two women so late in the game. We were unbelievably lucky.

Afterward we learned that the Germans were already blowing up the bridges; the closest to us was the Franz Joseph Bridge, named after the Austro-Hungarian emperor. I had used that one the most on the trolley to go to Pest where I was teaching English in Kobanya. In a fleeting moment I thought, how I will be able to teach when the war is over and transportation is crippled in the city? But where were we yet from that?

We stayed in the same building until the Russians, after house-to-house street fighting, conquered Buda on February 12, 1945, Pest was already occupied much earlier.

The large room we all gathered in during the bombing and was actually the property of Bozse, we finally vacated. Those who owned their own apartments now had to work on making them habitable again. Since the one we rented on a high floor was badly damaged by mortar fire, we decided to stay on the ground floor, and Bozse was happy to have help with the baby, whom mostly I took care of.

On February 12, after the siege that had lasted two months in Buda, we finally met the Russians face to face. We were very lucky. We found out quickly that the ones who entered the apartment were top officers with their company commander, and they set up their headquarters here, with all the telephones, telegraphs, and radios. They were the most civil army corps we could have hoped for. The first thing I did was to greet them and remove my watch from my wrist, handing it over as a gift. We had heard that the soldiers took away all the watches from the populace and that they were walking around with six, eight, ten watches on their arms. So I was not going to wait until they take it away from me. My courtesy impressed them, and they treated us with respect. My mother, being originally from Slovakia and since Russian was also a Slavic language, could speak with them, and they could understand each other. They brought in a lot of food (it was about time, I had lost twenty pounds!), and mother was cooking and baking for them and, of course, for us as well.

Finally we could go out on the street and walk around to see what damage was caused by all the shelling and the bombs. Were the stores reopening so people can buy essential things for their sustenance? But all this happened very slowly. The Russians drafted the men; as soon as they were walking around they picked them up and put them to work to clean the rubble, fix the pipes, restore the electricity, and dig up the sewer lines. Most of this was done with shovels and pickaxes—there was no large machinery in existence yet. The army trucks helped move the rubble away so the streets would be serviceable for the cars, trucks, and wagons. I saw such a wagon, which was packed full of stuff that the soldiers were looting from the residents. I asked the soldier for bread, and he pointed at the seat next to him—I should come up on the wagon. I ran away so fast. I had heard enough of the soldiers raping all the women, young and old, and I would not be one of them.

Meanwhile my mother was busy working for them. When she did not cook she was sewing up sheets to make the sacks that served to send the stolen goods back to Russia. They were in need of everything; the war with the Germans had devastated their country, their cities, and their homes. We were infinitely grateful to them for saving our lives. If not for these Russians, who knows if any Jews would have remained alive? They lost millions of their own people in this horrible world war fighting the Germans. What a waste; humanity suffered because of one maniac who could not be stopped. Hitler, as a young man, wanted to be an architect, but they did not take him in at the university in Austria. How much better off the world might have been had he not used his frustration creating World War II.

There were also offices opening up for the people to register those who stayed alive and to search for those who had not returned yet. So far we had not heard anything about my father or any of the others who had left at the same time with him. But we were still hoping...

I went to a nearby office that had opened and turned out to be the seat of the communist party in Buda. To my great surprise I met the leader, the same young man who came to visit his mother in the apartment I used to sublet from the old lady. She was the other tenant who worked at the Ritz as a cosmetician.

He recognized me and was very friendly. He asked me how we were doing, and when I told him that we are without funds and without food, he gave me a large sack of flour. I could hardly carry it home.

Then we had a big surprise. Tamas walked in with his right arm in a cast. How he found us I don't know. He was the first person who came to see us since we had left our home in Bajvivo street, before I moved to my sublet and before my parents left for the yellow-star house. It was almost surreal. Both mother and I were delighted to see him. When I voiced my concern about his arm, he told us that he had asked his doctor to do this; otherwise, the Russians would have put him to work on the streets with shovels that he had never used before in his life. There was nothing wrong with him. Very clever. Of course being a violinist he had to protect himself. When we asked him if he thought it would be time for us to move back to our old home, he assured us that it was OK.

After a while when it seemed safe enough to walk on the streets with all the construction going on, mother somehow got a cart big enough to pile our belongings on. Actually it was not much, and the two of us were pushing and pulling the cart from one end of Buda to the other. Once more we looked back at the buildings surrounding the Horthy Circle, saying good-bye to all the hardships we experienced here yet glad that here we saved our lives.

We did find the building standing and our apartment empty with all the windows broken except in the small maid's room and the kitchen. We learned from the janitor, who was the same person as when we left and now welcomed us returning to our home, that a German officer lived there until the retreat of the troops and that it was in fairly decent condition. We found our furniture intact and even some of our personal belongings in the closets.

The only thing we did not find were the wooden crates in the basement containing all the valuables we left there, including my whole trousseau that my mother slowly accumulated while I was growing up to have ready when I would get married. From linens and crystals to porcelain and silver, we thought that among all the other boxes of the residents those would be safe there too. But the Germans were smarter. They ordered every owner and tenant of the apartments to mark their belongings with their name and apartment number, and of course the ones that were not marked belonged to the Jews who had to move to the ghettos. Those were removed and sent to their homes in Germany. The same thing happened with our fur coats, which we left in cold storage. The ones that were not personally identified were taken away. My beautiful nutria fur coat! I hardly ever had the chance to wear it. But I had no tears left for "things." I was crying for all the family we lost and friends who never returned.

We had to start thinking about our future—how to get some money to buy food and other needs. We saw a wagon in front of our building and started to talk to the man, who turned out to be from a nearby village. We complained that we were hungry and could he give us advice about what to do. He said to go out to the villages and take linens, clothes, whatever we could, to barter for food. Then feeling sorry for us he gave mother one egg. Somehow she made a meal out of it for both of us. Then we started to look through our closets to see what we could sell. We fixed a bundle, which my mother took on her back, and she started out for the country. In two days she returned, exhausted but happy, bringing home as many provisions as she could carry.

We lived in the small room until sometime later the glass could be fixed on the windows. Transportation was still difficult with the bridges destroyed. The Russians built one pontoon bridge and later fixed the Margit Bridge so Buda and Pest were connected again, and slowly traffic could flow. This was the longest bridge; in the middle it is connected to Margaret Island. One end at Pest and the other end at Buda were still there and could be repaired by joining the center. All the other bridges were totally destroyed.

Our apartment on Bajvivo street was close to this bridge, but for now we had to use the only safe crossing, the pontoon bridge that the Russians had quickly put together. To rebuild the other bridges was a much larger undertaking, and it took a lot more time.

I learned about an important office, which opened in Pest, called the American Joint Distribution Committee. I presented myself to the office manager. I was confident with my English knowledge and also Hungarian shorthand and typing, and I knew I could be useful in such an office, which was busy helping the Jews returning to their homes, also some arriving back from deportation. The Joint (as we all called it for short) received money and truckloads of clothing from Switzerland and it was this office which was a distribution center to various Zionist organizations. This was a fantastic help to the Jewish people who lost everything in the war and helped them to start up their life again. They helped us immediately with food that I took home, and I got a steady job as a secretary with a good salary. Finally we could buy things that were most urgent and pay for the repairs needed in the apartment. I was also able to set up my mother with a group of women to knit socks, caps, gloves, and scarves from wool the Joint gave me. When the women finished working on them, they returned the finished items, which the Joint distributed among the needy. Then mother received more wool to continue. I also had my friend R. Juci's mother join the group. Juci had lost her father also, and they were badly in need of some help. Now "we were in business," as they say.

As soon as we were settled, we found out that Zsuzska, my cousin from Ungvar, arrived in Budapest and was housed in a school with other refugees. Mother and I went to look for her and luckily we found her in good condition. She had been deported to Auschwitz with her sister Gabi and their parents. She told us a terrible story about Gabi, who was not able to eat the awful food they gave them; she lost a lot of weight and had no strength left for physical work. The Germans separated them, and Zsuzska never saw her again. She did not know anything about her parents either. She was then taken to a small town in Germany and worked in a bomb factory in miserable conditions but was lucky to survive, and after being liberated by the Russians at Theresienstadt, she found her way to Budapest. Of course we took her home with us, but she did not stay too long. After a couple weeks she went to Prague to enter the university there. The Czechs offered students a stipend—not only were they free to study whatever subject they wanted but they also received food and lodging. I was sorry that she left. It was like finding a new sister.

It became known that people from abroad were looking for their relatives and put ads in the Hungarian newspapers with their names and addresses so the survivors could get in touch with them. I found such an ad that was sent by a cousin of my father looking for us. He lived in New York, in the Bronx. Of course I wrote him a letter right away and was wondering what kind of answer I would get.

The job at the Joint was very pleasant. The people around me were friendly, and I guess they appreciated finding someone with the exact knowledge and skills they needed. One day my immediate boss, Lilly, showed me a letter I wrote and asked why I left out all the "$"s. I told her that the letter was crossed over. She had a good laugh and explained to me that it was the dollar sign. I had to rewrite the letter to fill in all the dollar signs, which I did happily.

Often I heard hushed voices in the office talking about forming groups of people who wanted to leave Hungary. Of course I was curious and asked the director, who happened to be a man from Miskolc, Gr. Sanyi, to tell me what this was all about. With the help of the Joint they planned to take small transports by train to Vienna at night, illegally, and pay off the guards and the customs officers with drinks, cigarettes, and money to let our people through. So far they had been quite successful. I told him that I was very interested and that he should let me know when they assembled the next group. I would like to go to America. I figured I would have a good chance to go to a member of our family. He said that in the spring they would have more transports leaving and that he would let me know.

You might think this was an enormous decision to leave not only a country but a whole continent and travel to a far-off land from where it would not be so easy to return and to relatives I had never met and do not know. But this was made easy by all the hardships I had suffered, the consequences of the war all around me, the differences I had with my mother, which made my life harder, and a strong desire to get away from all of it and see a new world, a new way of life, new people, and new opportunities.

And now I will return to my actual diary, which continued the last day of the year 1945—

New Year's Eve.

CHAPTER V

New Year's Eve. I am sitting here next to the tile-stove keeping warm and looking back at the year gone by. What did 1945 mean? Last year at this time in Bozse's room we went to bed at six o'clock, in our clothes, because it was cold and because we did not know which moment we would have to jump up and run away. Then at six in the morning we were listening to the noise of the Russian bombs falling, the boom of the mortars and the drum-fire of the machine guns. Certainly this New Year's Eve is nicer. At that time I was praying that we should be liberated by January 17 and that should be my big birthday present. It turned out that my present was a potato pancake that my mother made honoring me on my twentieth birthday with the greatest, unprecedented luxury of the times—a potato pancake.

The Russians entered on February 12. This is where our first disappointment started. O how much we have expected from our liberation! A new life, new people, new principles. And meanwhile we forgot that the twentieth century remains only the twentieth century, man is only man, and the principles... better not to talk about them. This is why we endured through the war; this is what gave us strength to struggle to live, so that now it will be better, perhaps live better than others, having earned that right by our suffering. We were hungrier more, we felt colder more, we lived in privation more than those who plundered us, who stole everything from us for themselves.

Our greatest surprise and greatest happiness was to find our apartment and our furniture intact. From Ujbuda we were pulling a cart filled with our belongings, and now we could fill up our old nest and restore our dear home.

Buda is not what it was when I left Bajvivo Street; it did not attract me anymore. However, we had no money, and without money one is bound to the soil. Spring arrived and slowly the rubble disappeared, the streets were cleaned, people started drifting back, acquaintances met again, and families reunited, but we had no news of my father. And more and more we heard of those whom we would never see again. Slowly we grasped what happened while we lived isolated with eyes bound, trying to save our own, small, fallible lives. Millions of people perished, and hundreds of people were working risking their own lives to save other millions. And I was not among them. I could not even save my own father.

Now that the war is over, the thought to live alone became unbearable. Finally I wanted to get married. Perhaps it will be better somehow, because I just could not bear this uncertainty, aimlessness, and unemployment alone any longer. So far the war was an excuse for everything. Now that it is over I had to realize suddenly how unbelievably empty and shallow is my life. Bandi and Francis both called me, but I knew that is not what

I want, not what I aspire to. P. Gyorgy came to look us up, and I started to think about him; perhaps this will be good for me, this is what I always wanted—or rather what my mother always wished for. He invited mother and I to Cegled, where there was a large Russian quarter and a hospital. He worked there through the winter helping the wounded Russian soldiers.

Of course we ate at the barracks. There was no private restaurant functioning yet in the town, but my mother was upset that he, as a doctor, was not able to offer us something better than the troop's cafeteria. Meanwhile Gyorgy and I started talking about finding a nice apartment in Budapest if we were to consider our future together. So we decided to look around to see what is available, but they were all in terrible condition, damaged by the shelling and bombing, and it would take a lot of money to restore any of them. Since neither my mother and I nor Gyorgy had the means, he having lost his parents and living only on his own income now, we had to forget about this plan. Mother put an end to our speculation. I thought she would now be pleased that I have found a doctor, but I realized she also wanted one who is rich. So this was the end of it, and now there is no one else who came back to Budapest that I knew. My life did not change; it continued in the same old routine.

We learned the first sad news after the siege when we could walk outside—Robert had died. Toward the end the Arrow-Cross men were so violent that they emptied all the yellow-star houses and deported everybody. The Jews who tried to hide were in mortal danger, and even to go on the streets was life threatening. As mother and I were told, he felt that the safest place was in the lion's den. He moved to the Ritz Hotel, one of the hotels along the Danube where the SS officers stayed.

What he did not know, or even think of, was that they were also the most important target. The whole row of luxury hotels were carpet bombed by the English. The Germans went down into the basements, but he stayed alone in his room and he was killed. How many people's lives he saved and yet he had to perish! This is the first time it struck me: why was I one of the many whom he wanted to save?

I also found out that Gyuri died, if it is true. I could not find out how and what happened to him. He was taken with all the others toward the Russian front, and none of them ever came back. I still cannot believe it. And the question is even stronger in me now—why did I have to survive? When I was in Cegled visiting P. Gyorgy, and I saw that with this marriage I will not get what I wanted, not even half of what I would like to have, and it was Gyuri who stopped me. At that time I did not know anything about him. I am mourning him with all my heart and soul, and I will never get over it.

I was very happy when Zsuzska came to our home, as if a sister had returned. It was a pity that we could not stay longer together; she cheered up many of my hours when I had been lonely for so long.

When I finally found employment our situation improved a little, and we were better off financially. This also helped all the altercations between mother and me, although I could still not call it a real truce between us.

The last couple of weeks there were some British soldiers arriving to Budapest. Since I spoke English well, they were very friendly toward me. I helped them with their shopping since the city center was opening up with good stores and the best merchandise, and they were the ones who had the money to buy anything and everything. Mostly they wanted to send back some nice fashion pieces to their girlfriends and to their families. One nice young man from the air force wanted to buy me a beautiful pullover. I thanked him, but I did not want to become obligated to him in any way. Of course the result was that now, on New Year's Eve, I am alone instead of dancing with them somewhere.

So now I stand here at the start of a new year, again lonely as always, with a sad smile, longing for merry laughter, troubled and worried, feeling old but thirsting to be carefree and youthful. I am a bit curious what 1946 will bring me, but actually does it matter what it will bring if it will not bring back my father and Gyuri? I have one plan and one aim, perhaps because one cannot live without a purpose: I want to get away from here. I could not spend my life with such memories, in such an environment, where those who lived around me were the ones I loved, and now these people living here committed the worst crimes on innocent men, women, and children. When I sit in the trolley I cannot help thinking that the man next to me could be the murderer of my father...

I would like to provide my mom with all the basics, fill up her pantry, so that when I leave she will not be lacking for anything, and if I succeed to establish my life abroad (although I don't yet know how), then she could follow me. I told her about the transports that are leaving almost monthly, and with the help of the Joint I could go to America. She did not try to stop me but asked that I wait for the spring when all hardship is easier to manage. We started preparing things for the trip, checking out my clothes, what I could take that will serve me best in the coming months en route.

As for marriage I am totally disillusioned, and I am afraid of it like fire. There is not one man I can believe in, one who would be even a little bit suitable to me, who would love me truly... Oh Gyuri, why couldn't you have survived? The whole world would have benefited more from you more than from me. Once I thought I could be creative, accomplish great things, become famous! But I will go nowhere with my frankness in this cunning, hypocritical, selfish world. No matter. I know it will be difficult, but I have to try. "He who dares succeeds." So let's be off bravely to the New Year! It cannot be worse than 1945 was. So take it easy girl; it will be better once again.

Another surprise was Laci, my first cousin, the son of my father's older brother from Miskolc. We did not see him since we moved to Budapest and now wondered how he found us. He told us that he lost his sister and her little boy and his parents. He was now with some friends in Budapest, trying to find something to do. We discussed the possibility of going abroad, but I did not mention that I was actually working on a plan at my office.

Will I really succeed to leave by this spring? This is my only hope: to have the patience and endure this winter here. And what am I expecting after I escape from Hungary? Perhaps an even harder life and even more loneliness will wait for me there. All the same, at least I must try. "Fortune favors the brave!" So have courage and get on with 1946.

VIENNA, 1946. MARCH 17, SUNDAY

The departure happened quite suddenly. I was planning to leave at the beginning of April, but because of the confused state of affairs it seemed better to leave sooner. Quickly I threw everything together and packed all that I was taking with me.

When I told mom that I would like to travel now I was admiring her strength and, moreover, that she agreed with me. Poor woman. She was crying a lot, and her situation is really very difficult; she remains here all alone in Budapest.

I barely said good-bye to a few people, from Juci,...and interestingly I bumped into Sandor, Gyuri's best friend. I had not seen him for a long time, and just now fate threw him in my path. Even he did not know what happened to Gyuri. Then on my last day the mailman brought me a postcard from Tamas, which he sent from Buckarest some time ago. This is how I learned his address, and I quickly wrote him a letter that I am leaving.

I got a call that we are leaving March 15th at seven in the morning. We assembled at seven but the train started only at one o'clock. Mother was with me at the train station till eleven. She stood there, poor thing, and was watching me speechless, hungry and tired, but did not move, as if her legs could not carry her away from me.

At the end I could not even kiss her for the last time. Actually leaving would not have been difficult at all if I did not have to leave her here. I did not miss anybody and anything; I did not even look back. And so I boldly started out into the WORLD.

I left together with Laci. This happened by chance. We both have one aim, one goal, and we decided to stick together. Actually, my mother felt it is better for me to be with him than to go alone.

Travelling went relatively well. We got seats all the way and I slept through the whole night, which is saying a lot since I never can sleep on a train. I woke up because the train stopped, and it was standing on the rails for a long time. Russians were walking in and out; there was a big commotion, shouting, but finally all went quiet, they gave the order, and the train could leave. We passed through the border—we escaped our "prison!". After this we are free, wanderers of the world. We don't depend on anyone; no one will order us around. The train was flying with us toward a nicer, happier and freer future, which for the time being, however difficult, can only be better than the past.

It was nine o'clock in the evening when we arrived at the frontier station. We travelled eight hours by train. To think of it—my father trod this road all the way on foot!

We arrived in Vienna at three o'clock in the morning. It is a pity we travelled in the dark; I could not see the countryside. We remained on the train until the sun came up, and then we got on the trolley. As refugees we travelled free of charge.

It felt so good to see foreign people, to hear a foreign language, to read the Viennese signs, and to ask stupid questions with the privilege of a stranger. The first thing I learned was that a tram ticket costs twenty-five groschen, and that one cigarette is 2.5 to 3 schillings, which counts as one of the most expensive items here. I was glad to know this because the Joint gave me cigarettes for the trip and, since I did not smoke, I will be able to sell them and have some Austrian currency. When we arrived in the Rothshield Spital (the hospital), they took a census. We got vaccinated for typhoid, and then we were disinfected. In the morning we got coffee and before noon some milk, and everything was sweetened.

In the interim time I took care of my considerable correspondence, first to my mother, then to G. Sanyi, my boss in the office, and then to Tamas. A young man who was returning the same day took the letter to my mother with him. I hope she will receive it soon.

This large hospital was currently used only for the refugees. Our whole group settled down here until the time that the transport was able to continue on to the next stop. We could select our cots, women in one section, men in another, and we stretched out some sheets to separate us and to have some privacy. We also received our dinner here, which tonight was a delicious pea soup and a pastry with milk and raisins, all very sweet. Everything they give us is nutritious and good. After dinner Laci and I decided to go into town to look around. The city is old and suffered badly from the bombing. The Ring is very nice; the Rathouse, the Burg, and the Parlament are beautiful; and the Staatsoper must have been wonderful. Generally the public buildings are very impressive even though they were badly damaged.

It is really a great help that I speak German so well; it is easy to ask around and get directions so we don't get lost. Unfortunately Laci knows very little; he certainly has no talent for languages, so I have to help him with everything.

Vienna, 1946. March 19, Tuesday

I was compelled to stop to join the others, and am writing now only because of the many programs here. We are called to various activities, meetings, meals, snacks, etc. and of course it is fun to get to know people around us.

I familiarized myself with Vienna thoroughly; it is large, old, and full of ruins. The important public buildings are very beautiful. The Viennese are incomparably more polite and neat than the people in Budapest; on the other hand, the city is completely desolate, and you cannot get anything at all in the world. There is no merchandise anywhere; the stores are empty. I had a hard time finding a place where I could have my hair done, and I wanted to get a permanent. I sold a couple of cigarettes, and now I don't know what to do with my money.

The company around us is quite good. By chance I met B. Jozsi, whom I had met before the war with his younger brother when I travelled with my father to Varna in 1939. He told me that his brother Imre was shot dead. This was shocking news—shocking to me only because it was someone I knew and had very dear memories of. He was my age. Many times we learned that the Jews were lined up on the Margit Bridge, and they fell into the Danube when they were shot. So now I meet Jozsi again; like me, he also is leaving his past behind. We became very friendly; he is a pleasant person. .

Otherwise I am with Americans. There was a Purim Ball on Sunday night, which is where I met them. They are trying to persuade me to stay here; I could have a good job with them, room and board, and a good life. What I would have given to have such an offer in Budapest! Here it does not attract me though; Vienna is dead and boring, and I have absolutely no desire to remain at the very first stop and settle down. This is not why I started out and left everything behind. With their help I did send a telegram to New York City to my relatives. I got an American cap from them and a couple of badges; perhaps I will be able to use them somewhere, you never know.

I go out with them to dinner and dancing, and they took me around Vienna by car. I receive chocolates and cigarettes from them, and they really try to please, but I think I can get the same elsewhere too.

I was in wonderful spirits during the first days. I felt liberated like never before. During the ball, men who worked for UNRRA (United Nations Relief and Rehabilitation Administration) were handing out chocolates, cookies, and prunes, and even though we did not have any drinks, we were in a very good mood among this international company, I already forgot during the war years, what life is like, when different nationalities meet and exchange their thoughts and opinions. Generally I find life here very interesting.

VIENNA, 1946. MARCH 24, SUNDAY

We are still in Vienna. It has already been eight days that we have been here. The four "Great Powers" divide the city: Americans, English, French, and Russians. Our part is under the Russians, and they now closed the border, so we cannot continue on to the next stop. We were the next-to-last group who left Hungary. How lucky we were that we made it! It was so important that we got here, and from Vienna we will be able to move on, hopefully soon. Perhaps they will take us toward Munich.

We are completely bored with Vienna; we already visited all the nightclubs (where the most you can get is a raspberry drink). I saw the Fledermaus and Pick Dame in the opera, and I went to see the Prater with the Americans, which was so famous and now it is in ruins. I was also in the well-known thermal bath, called Diana Bad.

I became quite fluent in German; last night I was able to enjoy a cabaret, which I had always wanted to see. It had an act that was a literal, political, and social satire with such fantastic actors, the likes of which I had not seen for a long, long time. After the show I was dancing here in our building. (The UNRRA is very decent that they see to it that we even have a place to dance.) However, a number of us have had enough of all this by now. The enthusiasm of the first days diminished, and again my impatient nature is asserting itself to move forward. Let's go, move on, move ahead!

I wonder if I will have this urge to move all my life. Or will I succeed in settling down somewhere, where I will find my tranquility? G. Juci is already expecting a child, M. Agi perhaps already has a baby and I am living my infertile life, which seems almost aimless, at least for the moment, and is in no way satisfactory. It would have been good to remain together with Zsuzska; I would have someone with whom I could truly, candidly, and without any reservation or sense of fear, share my thoughts. Poor girl—she too is all alone, yet she also tries to find her place in this world.

It looks like the Americans dropped me as a companion. By the time they noticed that they are running after the wrong wagon, there is nothing to gain here. They think they should not over exert themselves, so they stayed away. As If I would miss them! It was nice while it lasted, and I practiced my English with them and enjoyed all the entertainment that Vienna has to offer. Of course this was very limited, but considering that it is so soon after a world war, I fully understand it and am not complaining.

What shall I do with Jozsi? They want to go to Bruxelles. He is together with a lot of nice young men, smart and capable, and perhaps their acquaintance could be very useful to me. I cannot know yet where my journey will take me. Should I consider to travel with them?

Laci is a fairly good partner; we understand each other well, and we laugh a lot—and that's exactly what I need. Sometimes he reminds me of my father, there is such likeness between them. I can almost see him in front of me. My poor father. I wish he could see me here now. How he would have enjoyed the Fledermaus together with me. It was his favorite How he would have shown me around Vienna! Jozsi also reminds me of him—the times we travelled together to Sofia, Varna, Istanbul. Somehow now I feel his absence even more than in Budapest. In Pest one was only toiling away; here there is time to think. And my mother and I were still waiting for him to come home…

I don't know why or from what, but my legs started swelling. I got very concerned and looked up the doctor, who was quick to settle the matter. He listened a little to my heart and gave me two pills. I am to put my legs up at night. That's all. A fine thing, but what if there is something wrong with my heart? He said I should rest more, but that is exactly what I don't like to do and certainly this is not the time to do it. I would rather live ten years less, but I cannot watch out for myself. Especially now, when I have started on a road where I am really not in control. I have to go wherever they take me and at the time when we are told to go.

Our group is studying Hebrew. I also started studying with them but went along only for the first lesson. Somehow it did not interest me. I already studied Hebrew in school, and I could read it, but I did not understand it as a living language; to me it was more like a prayer. My purpose is so different. I decided that I will open a group to teach them English. I wonder how far I can get them to advance.

VIENNA, 1946. APRIL 4, THURSDAY

Vienna…still in Vienna. I'm bored stiff, and I'm edgy; I don't even want to hear about why we are encircled and how much longer we will have to wait. It is now the third week that we have been sitting here, and by this time the circumstances are becoming unbearable. The Russians won't open the border; there are negotiations, but they don't tell us anything about it. I am tired of the people around me, the building where I live, the bed where I sleep, the atmosphere, the Jews. So many Jews together in one place is not easy to take. So far I have been waiting patiently that something should happen to us. But now I have had enough.

I went to all the American offices until I managed that possibly on the eighth we will receive a pass, and with that we can proceed individually. I wish I would have thought of this sooner. At least now we have some hope. Either the transport will go first, or we will by ourselves.

When I say "we," I mean with Laci. When I had to request the papers I had to do it for him too—he was unable to do much for himself. My mother thought that having Laci next to me would be very helpful, but instead it is the other way around. He is the one who gained everything since I arranged for him to join the transport, and now I also have to help him with all the official business that is necessary on this trip.

By now they ran out of our food supply. The appropriation became inadequate because there are too many of us. I am tired of eating powdered scrambled eggs. When I got to the point of total despair, I ran into a soldier from Palestine, the one I met at the Purim Ball. He helped us out with bread and jam, and I even got some dates from him. Looks like there are still some nice people around. He also gave me a lot of addresses that may be helpful later in our journey.

I still heard no news from my mother. Had I known that we would stay here for so long, would I have done things differently? It is good sometimes to idle one's time away, but this by now is too much. And I am not teaching the English group either; I have no patience for it.

My legs are not swelling anymore. I don't know what it was from, even though I tire myself out much more now, but there is nothing wrong.

I do not see the Americans anymore. These men! All men are interested until they get a girl, or they find out they can't get one. At that point their interest comes to an end.

The first group arrived from Budapest, and they still do not take us farther. Dear God, on the 16th of March how rapturously happy we were, what joy and freedom was throbbing in us! And now this feeling has deflated in little over two weeks. We wish to go on, to go farther! I am afraid that all my life it will be like this. It is only good as long as there is an aim ahead of me, and as soon as I reach that aim, I again desire something else and am never satisfied. I wonder if America will satisfy my wishes, and I will be able to finally settle down.

Will people in my social circle be like these irresponsible, thoughtless, superficial, light men and women I met here? Or are there serious, intelligent, cultured people there too, who in the true sense of the word are "gentlemen"? Will I be lucky enough to meet such people? I must trust in my own luck that, so far, was always with me. America is so big, and I know so little about it. Sometimes just thinking about it frightens me.

Recently something interesting happened when I bumped into a photographer from Budapest. I had worked for two weeks for E. Zaugg, a journalist. He took me to dinner; and when I asked him for ten dollars for my work, he only wanted to give me one American dollar. I did not accept it, and I wrote him a letter, which he "would not put in his window," (could not brag about it, as they say). He then referred me to a Mr. Kublin, who would settle the matter with me. While in Budapest, I did not have any more time to bother with this because I left so suddenly. And here I bump into this photographer, who turns out to be Mr. Kublin. He announced that in accordance with Zaugg's instructions, he has to pay me five dollars. He wanted to give my only three, but I did not accept it. However, it turned out that he has Swiss watches with him, which Zaugg sent him from Switzerland, where he is presently. Since Laci already wanted to buy a watch in Budapest, he jumped at the chance and bought a watch for eight dollars—dirt cheap—and I also got my five dollars. Laci bought two more watches from him; one he sold, and the other he kept almost for free with the money he made.

Such is pure chance!

SALZBURG, 1946. APRIL 16, TUESDAY

Unbelievable! Suddenly we were on the way to Salzburg. Yesterday we arrived at 3:30 in the afternoon by bus. It was a beautiful drive. I was standing all the way in the front of the bus enjoying the countryside. It is marvelous. Spring is here, green buds are quivering on the trees, and some flowers are peeking out of the ground. Nature is so beautiful; even a war cannot spoil it. The transport is very well organized We have no worries; we even get full board and are brought to places by car. If only the Jews would be a bit different. I find most of them here ungrateful, demanding, impolite, and pushy, Instead of appreciative and hopeful.

I want to write a bit more here about the four weeks "on vacation" in Vienna. Since the border was closed, all the transports were stopped too. This way at least I had a chance to have a good look at Vienna and its surroundings. We were hitchhiking to Kahlenberg and Leopoldsbergen, in Schonbrunn, everywhere in the company of Americans or the British; we visited all the bars, though you could not get anything but lemonade unless the Americans and the British brought some drinks with them. Here I ate the first orange and the first peanuts I had ever had. On the Ring I met M. Gabi with his wife, the brother of Tamas. It turned out that the last two weeks we had lived together in the Rotschield Spital, and we did not even know it. We now sent Tamas a joint letter. Gabi and his wife live in a kibbutz, and they want to go back. It is interesting to observe the coincidences all along the trip. We parted from our group in Vienna. I did not see them anymore..

We left at dawn on Sunday by train. We travelled comfortably in a very wonderful compartment and also got food for the road. I sang by the window of the train all during our trip. We travelled through beautiful country and arrived to the town of Enns by the afternoon, where we received supper and slept there overnight. The next morning it was on to Salzburg, this time by car. We almost missed the car, but by skipping breakfast and the package of food they gave out, we caught it and by the afternoon arrived in Salzburg. This time Laci was helpful—he pushed me up on the car just in time.

I cannot admire the snowcapped mountains enough here. I am only sorry that all day we were waiting around to make sure we will continue our trip and did not have time to go on an excursion. At five in the evening we are leaving again by car, crossing the Austrian-German border into Munich. People I talked to all tell me not to go toward Italy because from there the plan is to go to Palestine. From Munich I will be able to manage my case better to continue to America. I wrote to my relatives in the Bronx; I hope they will do everything to get me over there. I have a lot of trouble with Laci. He is so aggressive, sometimes even with small matters, that he embarrasses me by his behavior. My nature is so different from his. Yet we have to stay together; otherwise I would be very much alone.

We were traveling together with B. Jozsi, and it was good to have a friend beside me. One time, by accident, my group was left behind, and his group was able to leave sooner. It is possible that at the next station we may meet up again, however. We missed the transport, and again I was reminded that I should only trust myself. Nothing is impossible when I manage my own affairs.

Otherwise, I must admit, I don't miss anyone from home, not even my mother. It feels so good to be independent and free, that I don't belong to anyone and don't have to adapt to anyone. I do worry about mother, though; I still have no news from her. If I knew that she is well and is taken care of, I would have no problems. I wonder if the knitting shop is still working and it brings in enough income for her to maintain her living standard.

MUNICH, 1946. MAY 3, FRIDAY

We were only two days in Salzburg. It is a pity—such a nice city and so much to see, but we had to go on with the others to Ainring, which is in Germany. Ainring is so far the best camp, with nice clean barracks built of wood and central heating. These used to be the barracks of the troops at the airport. Now it serves as a depot to gather the refugees of the war until they can go home or wherever... We were four in a small room. It was quite pleasant. The surroundings were beautiful; there were enormous snow-covered mountains that circled the small valley where Ainring was situated. I almost felt like I was in Switzerland. I went into the office to register, and they wanted to keep me there to work with them. They offered me a salary and lodging. I could stay for a couple weeks, but I did not want to stay here for long. I wanted to settle down finally and choose a fixed place from where I can correspond with my relatives and I can manage the fastest way out of Europe. After all, this is my goal.

I came into Munich today to look around, perhaps to find a job, but it happened to be Easter Friday, and we found everything closed. I could not accomplish much. We went out to the headquarters of UNRRA where by chance I made the acquaintance of two captains. One was very nice; he gave me a lot of chocolate, soap, a comb, etc., and he warned me that I should not go to work for UNRRA because "secretary" also meant something else. This young man was the most decent American I have met so far. He wrote, that is, sent a telegram, to our relatives in New York, mine on my father's side and Laci's on his mother's side. Unfortunately he was later transferred and now I don't know if the telegram was answered.

I am waiting with excitement because ever since I got their letters in Hungary—when they wrote that they will be helping me with everything—I have received no other news from them at all so far. The other captain was less helpful. He was a true lady's man who always runs after the girls and is totally spoiled by the European women. After all, they got used to the fact that the women will do it even for a cigarette. Of course none of them can understand that I am not "modern" enough. Too bad.

In Munich we found out that the first ship leaves for America on April 28. It is most important that at least the emigration has started. We arrived just at the right time. When I returned, Jozsi also arrived back in Ainring. It was nice of him that before we finally parted he came to say good-bye. By now he is probably in Bruxelles. Who knows if in this life we will ever meet again? In any case it would be interesting to meet in seven years. (It was seven years ago when we first met on the ship on the Danube.)

After the Easter holidays we came into Munich again, and after serious deliberation, I took a job at the American Joint Distribution Committee (looks like the Joint is my fate). I got a nice letter of recommendation from Gr. Sanyi saying that I worked with them in Budapest, which I presented here in their Munich office. They immediately offered me the job, no questions asked. I still don't know if my decision was the right one. Through them I got a beautiful small room where I can live together with Laci. We registered ourselves with the police and received our food stamps together with the extra stamps—refugees were entitled to more than the Germans. (This is the first time I feel a special privilege over others.) Then we returned to Ainring for our bags.

In Salzburg I had received a good skirt and a dress. I was altering the dress, sitting outside in the sun and dressed in shorts, when the UNRRA camp director approached me. When he heard how well I speak English, he asked me if I would want to work in their offices. I would receive UNRRA uniform and everything that goes with it. He wondered where I had been hiding so far, "such an attractive girl and speaks English so well."

After one hour he returned with his superior and another man from UNRRA. They are both handsome young men. One is a major. To make a long story short, since I was dressed in shorts and not a skirt or dress, they took me sunbathing, then in the evening we went to dance in the Reihenhall, which was the officers' club. They even had my dress ironed, since I could not obtain an iron to do it myself. To tell the truth, I was a little apprehensive to go with them, but in the end I had a great time. I had fun with all three men and, needless to say, I did not stay overnight with any one of them. I did not accept the position, and the next day we moved to Munich for good.

During our first trip to Munich while returning back to the camp, we boarded the American car by mistake and had a wonderful time. We pretended in front of the German conductor to be Americans. Next day we went to Berchtesgaden. Because we missed the train in the morning, we stood on the highway hitchhiking and got there by car. This way it was even more fun.

In Munich our first business was to apply for emigration to America. We again sent telegrams to our relatives. Of course we did not know any of them; we only knew that they existed through our parents' correspondences. After that I was running around for two days until I arranged the apartment, the food stamps, and the police. My greatest enjoyment was when the Germans were queuing up in the offices; we, on the other hand, could go in at once.

I did not think too long about taking the job at the Joint, and I don't know if I did the right thing or not. As far as the work, it is good, because I learn a lot. I do English shorthand and typing, and I do the correspondence. However, I miss a social life; I have no company at all. After office hours I always sit at home, cook supper, and do some sewing. Generally I enjoy this small home, which I established so soon by myself. And our sustenance is good, so I cannot complain. I must say that I can hold my own as well as any man, and at this moment I even provide 100 percent for Laci too. I hope I will be successful in America at least to the same degree as here. Of course I don't mean that I would want to support a man; I just wish to establish my life on the same standard that I have been used to.

I don't want to be a secretary—I have much higher ambitions. It is nice what I accomplished here in such a short time, but I don't consider this a real achievement. I want much much more than this. I want to excel, to rise above the others, not to be only one among many. And perhaps all will turn out well. After all, life truly just started for me now. It is only here that the borders opened up for me, and opportunities are unfolding in front of me for the first time.

I am thinking of Gyuri a lot. Now that I met a lot of men, not one of them measured up to him even a little bit. Laci and I often talk about the future and about marriage, which seems so distant and unimaginable and somehow also appears like it would be some sacrifice on my part. On the other hand, I am longing more and more to have a child, one I could coddle, love, bring up, and take care of.

As long as the goal, America, is ahead of me, I am the most balanced person on earth. I don't remember ever being like this before. I wonder if when I get there and reach that goal, will I have a new aim worth fighting for, or will an immense disappointment await me?

I think I should not be disillusioned so much because at worst I will move on.

This is a big world.

MUNICH, 1946. MAY 14, TUESDAY

At night I dreamed about Gyuri. It was not true that he died. He arrived and came to see me, and we went to the registry office for a marriage license. Mr. M was our witness. When my mother learned about it, of course she was very angry, and her behavior with Gyuri was so nasty that even my dear Aunt Szeren, who was also present, tried to counterbalance the situation with her kindness. I just bought a large package for mother from here in Germany, and among the things in it was half a kilo of orange marmalade, her favorite, which I was ready to give her. But because of her behavior I changed my mind and did not hand it over. I don't have to mention what a painful disappointment it was to wake up after such a dream when I was so happy to be with Gyuri again. He was a famous person, and when someone wanted to see if it was really him who was such a great artist, then Gyuri, with five or six lines, drew a face that was so splendid he immediately justified his great talent.

1946. June 1, Saturday

The month of May went by swiftly. It was not as nice as it could have been…or such as I would have liked May to be. I am alone as always, I cannot find my match; in fact, I can say that I cannot even find a suitable partner…because I am not modern enough and I am afraid to live. I was down twice in Ulm, visiting Guth. He is a very nice man, and I spent a few very pleasant hours with him. Through him I received two letters from Uncle Max. It is a good feeling to know that someone is waiting for me on the other side of the world. He wrote me that he already arranged my boat ticket to New York City and that my mother will pay him back the amount of the ticket to his wife's (Malvin) relative in Budapest. Not a bad idea. So far I did not know anything about this, so it is a pleasant surprise for me.

Today, Saturday, I have a day off. I am free as a bird and I have no programs. One of the young men from Ainring wanted to come to see me, but I don't like to be tied down when the person is not interesting enough—it is not worthwhile. So I excused myself with a pretext. However there was another person who was more fascinating. My case is handled by HIAS (Hebrew Immigration Aid Society), and I met a Belgian there who at once took a liking to me and who promised to take my case into his hands, that is, he will attend to my emigration. And then he invited me for dinner. By now knowing how men are thinking, I told him that I will be very pleased to spend a pleasant evening with him, but I am telling him in advance that I will not be his girlfriend. In spite of this we met in the evening and I received a beautiful French scarf from him. I can say that truly I had such an evening like I only had long ago. You could tell that he is European, cultured, intelligent, a versatile person. Next morning he came to my office and brought me a book about which previously we had spoken: Jean Giono's *Le Chant du Monde*. The book is indeed beautiful. I am glad to read it in French. It is gratifying that I do not forget this language, so far a had no opportunity to practice it. (This book would suit both Gyuri and me). So far I did not hear from the Belgian, maybe he is traveling and is away from Munich.

Meanwhile life goes on smoothly; our meals are very good, though I dislike the Joint including all their people there. It was much nicer in Budapest, where everybody was very friendly. I am bored in Munich and am waiting patiently and passively for something to happen.

There was a recent incident worth recording. Last evening I stayed in the office late trying to finish some work, and by the time I left, the trams were not running anymore. So I started to walk home when I saw an American jeep and I figured I would hitchhike because it was too dark to walk alone. The jeep stopped and three black American soldiers were sitting in it. I had to make a quick decision: do I say no thank you or do I get in? The driver pointed to the front seat and I joined them. They were surprised that I spoke perfect English; they were very polite, and I told them that my husband is anxiously waiting for me. He will be very upset that I get home so late, but I was tied up in the office and had no transportation. I explained to them where we lived and they took me to the door. Thanking them profusely I ran into the building with a sigh of relief…that I got away with it. Until then I had never met any black people face to face; of course, in Hungary they did not exist.

MUNICH, 1946. JUNE 24, MONDAY

It is cold. I am sitting here in a warm, winter dress with the windows closed, and I wish I could be next to a fireplace. This is Bavaria. I pledged to myself that I will never come here again in my life. I just found out that the Belgian has left, but first he took care of the CJC clearance, which is essential in all this running around. It is my fault that when I finally meet someone I like and who is superior to all the others, I cannot loosen up, show him that I appreciate him, and say that I would like to stay in touch with him. Now I may have lost him forever.

We have to wait to get on the quota and receive our visas. I learned that the quota with which we can go to America is for orphans, so we can enter legally. It is very difficult for me to wait since time is going by slowly, doing nothing, and the new life, the new beginning, seems almost out of reach. And unfortunately I have no one I could shift some responsibility onto, responsibility of my own life. Also I am impatient. I should be happy that we came this far in a relatively short time.

I finally received some news from my mother. She is a great problem for me. How will I be able to have her brought out now, when she did not come with me? On the other hand, I am glad she is not with me. I am much more liberated without her. My friend Juci wrote me also. She has a problem about whether to get married or not to a 39-year-old man whom she hates and is short and ugly but very rich. Well there are also problems like these. She lost her father too, and they really have a hard time managing. I arranged before I left to have her mother belong to the group with my mother where they are knitting for the Joint, but she has two aunts, her mother's sisters, who also lost everything during the war and now have absolutely no livelihood. The truth is that they are selling Juci to a rich man so they can profit by it. She is such a good, gentle soul; I feel sorry for her. Before I left I offered her to join me going to America, but of course her mother did not let her.

I had a pleasant surprise when my cousins Zsuzska and Robi came to visit me. They accidentally met in Prague at the university, she from Ungvar, he from Kassa. They received my address from mother and decided to make the trip. The refugees were moving around on the trains and did not even have to pay. We spent a couple of nice days together and then they returned to Prague. How different Zsuzska's nature is from mine! I feel she will find happiness much sooner than I will. Robi was also in Budapest during the deportation and was active in the underground movement fabricating false papers to save the Jews. He was caught by two detectives and was beaten badly but managed to escape. He was telling me about the men who were taken from the yellow-star houses by truck and then had them go on foot toward the Austrian border. The ones who were older and too weak were shot. He did not know that my father was probably one of them.

It would have been so much easier to melt into a kibbutz and rave about Eretz Yisrael with pure idealism. At age 16 this would have been perfect for me if my mother would not have killed this spirit in me. How many things have changed and formed my life and my mentality? I wonder, is everything very simple, or do I just not understand? It would serve me well to study psychology in America, if only to understand myself better. Anyway I must study something; I am young and ignorant, and only I know how ignorant indeed. In America the universities are free. It is of utmost importance how I start once I set foot over there. My whole life, my surroundings, my marriage, depends on this first step. Shall I possess the right instincts at the moment of my arrival? Because I can trust only my instincts, I cannot trust others.

MUNICH, 1946. JULY 1, MONDAY

I am writing with a new pen that I bought on route to Garmisch for fifty allied marks, which means five dollars, since I lost mine on the way to Frankfurt. Traveling a lot, right? To travel is the nicest thing in life, and one can never travel enough. We made the trip to Frankfurt because Laci was to get an affidavit there, but we did not find it. Anyway it is not essential. I traveled in the American compartment because the German section was so crowded that Laci could hardly get in there. Frankfurt is quite a nice big city with attractive white trollies and full of handsome American officers, well, also with unpleasant Germans, of course, as is all of Germany. It is dreadful how I hate them because I can attribute all bad things to these despicable people: my father, Gyuri, the destroyed six years of my youth, that I left my home and am now drifting alone in the world, not to mention millions of lives lost. Hitler alone could not have done that if the German people were not behind it.

Yesterday and the day before I was in Garmisch-Partenkirchen. I had a beautiful weekend with a very pleasant American second lieutenant, John V. We were in a villa where three officers currently live. It was a beautiful home—what life people must have lived here before the war. He is the first who was interested in my future and asked me to write to him. Garmisch is divine. We travelled to the Zugspitze on a train through a tunnel that is more than four thousand meters long and from there in a cable car (first time in my life) to the highest point. Tiny people were skiing in the snow below; someone made a beautiful Mogen David with his boots. Around us were the high peaks of the mountains of Switzerland, Austria, and Italy. Further down, the blue Eibersee can be seen with small green spots in it, and a sailboat is gliding on it barely visible to me. The sun is blinding our eyes, and black birds are strolling on the snow, picking up some crumbs. I wonder why they live so high up. Isn't life nicer in the green valley below where right now the air is fragrant from the flowers and fruits? Or were they ostracized by so many rivals that banished them into the higher regions?

MUNICH, 1946. JULY 3, WEDNESDAY

Laci left to visit his girlfriend, a German woman whose husband did not return from the war. I even gave him money to buy her flowers; he has no means to earn anything here and is totally dependent on me. I find this an interesting life. We live in one home like the best married couples (though this is not the type of husband I would imagine for myself), yet he has a girlfriend and I am going out with other men. As much as I am with them! I am a real coward; I am afraid to live, to live well! And life is so short.

Our emigration is advancing splendidly. We will have to move into the Funk Fort, and there is only one difficult step still to come: the Consul. After that we can go. One can turn gray having lived through the war—and now to struggle with the difficulties of this emigration!

In addition the whole world is in revolt. There are pogroms in Miskolc, rioting in Palestine. Today the Jews were fasting everywhere and held strikes demanding to change the orders by the English who stop the boats entering Palestine. When I hear these things I can only wonder what the answer is to our problem; one must not be a Jew, must not remain a Jew, because it only means persecution and unhappiness through generations. At the moment we as Jews enjoy an advantage here in Germany, but at what cost? And when we finally will be out of here, there could be new problems. I wonder if there is such anti-Semitism in America? And Jews have such an unfortunate nature; we are drawn to each other. When I mingled among Americans and I chose one man in the party, he always turned out to be a Jew. We are different people, more serious, with deep feelings and affinities, a keen intelligence, and we invite jealousy in others. Nothing can be done about that; it can't be helped.

How interesting life can be; how surprising are some things that somehow have to happen.

Yesterday I went to the HIAS office to take care of some documents when I met G. Vera, Gyuri's younger sister. She got married and came here with her husband. And we had to meet! She was sweet and charming as always. I liked her a lot, better than her older sister, Magdi. Of course we were talking about Gyuri. She told me the story that at one time, long ago, when she was a little girl, she got up at six in the morning and crept out of bed to read the letters that I wrote to Gyuri. And once, later, Gyuri found out and spanked her for it. She could never forget that. When we parted she wished me lots of luck. She said, "You will have to marry there a very nice American. Our Gyuri loved you very much." All day this meeting depressed me enormously. If God would have Gyuri come home and he would go boldly out into the world, he not even knowing where I am, yet I am sure we would meet. But regretfully there is no hope for that. Vera...she is a bit of Gyuri. If Gyuri would know what I still feel toward him, and if he would know that he was one of the principal reasons why I left my home, a place I wish to be as far away from as possible. I could not imagine my life in Budapest without him.

MUNICH, 1946. JULY 15, MONDAY

On the thirteenth one transport left, and we were left behind. By now I do not have any hopes for our early departure, and I try to prepare myself for the worst. I should have arranged my life in Munich better; of course one always sees this only in retrospect. I always thought that we are leaving soon. I left my job at the Joint and did not look for another. True, it was Laci who did not let me because it would have meant being tied down too much. He instead decided to sell some of his jewelry to have some money. The UNRRA luckily is still providing us with food, and we have everything we need and are living well.

It is quite interesting how we are together; I feel I should write about it. We became good friends. I candidly told him everything about myself, so we have no walls, no inhibitions between us, and we can discuss everything easily. He finally expressed his appreciation for all that I have done for him. Alone he would never have made this trip, and he can really thank me that he will get to America. He promised to buy me a mink stole, once he was established and he made some money. I do not take him seriously though; people promise all kinds of things and then they "forget" to actually do it. Now he left to spend the night with his girlfriend, and I remained alone. It was I who insisted that he continue with this affair; I thought it for the best. A man must live with a woman; otherwise, he is nervous and impossible to be with.

Yesterday we were in Murnau. We were swimming in a beautiful lake at the foot of the snowcapped mountains and took a sunbath on a small abandoned island until we returned home completely tanned like gypsies. I swam at least three kilometers; I did not know that I was capable of that distance. Laci followed me on a rowboat, but I needed no help. Then I took the oars from him, and I was rowing back under the pinewoods in the dusk. The stormy wind raised the waves high, my palm blistered from the oars, and I got tired, but even so, it felt good. Soon the Evening Star appeared, and the full moon came out. It was beautiful.

Now that I was not working I decided to take advantage of my time and get to know Munich better. It is a big city, but terribly damaged—there are hardly any buildings that were not in ruins from the heavy bombing by the Americans. Through Laci's girlfriend I met some other German girls; very few had their men back home. They took me to the Isar River and we raced to see who will reach the other side faster. I was not familiar with the water and was surprised how hard I had to fight the strong flow of the river to reach the other bank. I got to the other side at a much lower point than the others and had to walk back to meet them. The girls were friendly toward me, and of course it helped that I spoke German so well. One of the girls told us that she baked a cake and invited us to her home. I had not had homemade cake for a very long time, and I enjoyed her hospitality.

MUNICH, 1946. AUGUST 2, FRIDAY

Finally I achieved this too... We are traveling on the sixth to Bremen. I am counting the days since the 25th of July—that is when we went to the Consul. Actually everything went so nice and smoothly: I had so much luck all the way, everywhere we went. (I should not say it too soon.)

Major Butler...this is a name I will never forget. He was the most decent, nice man I met. I can thank him for everything. And with this my travel through Germany is ending. From emigration out of Europe I will change to my immigration to America. We will get on the train on Tuesday at two o'clock, and we will wait for the ship in Bremen. Within ten days I will set my eyes on New York. To pronounce "New York" sounds terribly strange. A New World, new life, new people, new relatives. I wonder what it will be like. Will I find a peaceful life where there is great hustle and bustle and restlessness? That I have reached this...I can thank Gyuri. He chased me from my home because he did not come back, and without him I did not want to live there. Here I met quite a lot of people, though regrettably I did not like any of them and none made any impression on me. Or it is possible that I am single minded, where nothing is important, neither amusement nor men and love, only my goal? And now I reached it. It is so unbelievable, that I am afraid to think of it, as if it were only a dream, I wonder that perhaps something is still not in order, perhaps some paper is still missing, or perhaps we still are awaiting a doctor's examination and we will not be permitted to leave.

I think when I finally get there; I will need at least a month of rest before I start, before I set a new goal in front of me: a career. I know it will be difficult; I know I will not be happy simply because I was not born for happiness. But I would like to say that when with grey hair I will look back, I will be able to smile with a calm satisfaction that it was worthwhile to live...I have accomplished something. Whether this will be in relation to the family or within the boundaries of mankind will be determined by my strength, my talent, and my luck. I have something in me that I want to show first of all to my mother and then to the other people who knew me in Hungary. But there is even something else, something more: was Gyuri right when he said that I am worth more than the others, that I cannot allow myself to become marshy? When I used to be a great idealist I would have liked to help people. The way I see it now, not all people deserve the kindness that a person would lavish on them. Mankind is bad and doesn't even want to become better. But no one can change me if I myself don't want to change; only the one who tries to change me will be ruined by my behavior. Gr. Sanyi wrote to me that I should use my luck to help others. Why and how should I help other people with whom I feel no fellowship? Not even at the cost of common suffering. I do not like many of them, even if they suffered more than I did because they are totally different from me, and they actually clash with me. These refuges can be fresh, aggressive, noisy, and ungrateful. What could I do with them?

BREMEN, 1946. AUGUST 9, FRIDAY

Just before leaving Munich in the last minute I received the photograph of Gyuri from his sister Vera. She was so nice to go out of her way to make sure I get it. I finally have a good picture of him. Will this mean even more pain having him always in front of me?

Here in Bremen I am sitting in the reading room, a quiet place, where I am almost afraid to bite into the apple, it makes such noise. I have been here one day. I got this far. I have not seen such a nice camp, brilliantly clean everywhere with white sheets on the beds, everything done with the American system. If people would not steal so much, every camp could look like this. Last night they were showing us a film about America, the land of freedom and democracy, where people are happy and live without inhibitions, where if you are working you can find wealth everywhere, and everybody can find what they are searching for. "This is my America and also it is yours." I was really touched by these words, and only now did I grasp what my voyage meant to "sail for America" into the New World, there to take roots, become one and the same with so many happy, ambitious, and carefree people, be part of a rich, large country, where one can travel thousands of kilometers and still be "at home." It is an extremely moving thought that finally one can be free from so much suffering—this awful pressure in Europe, where one is connected only to painful or terrifying memories—and from now on everything can and will make one happy.

Now I can enjoy every trifle, such as the ice cream, the likes of which I have never tasted that I ate today here in Bremen at the ice cream parlor. This place belongs to the American military base, but I walked in as if I were a WAC (Women's Army Corps), and since my English was perfect, no one questioned me. The women were not all wearing uniforms. I was watching what others were ordering, since it was all foreign to me, and I said, "the same." It turned out to be a milkshake, which in Hungary did not exist. It was delicious!

We have to wait here for two weeks for the ship, but now I am willing to wait patiently and gladly because I know I will be going. And the camp is so nice; it is a pleasure to live in it. The beds are comfortable, the bathrooms are luxurious, and here you do not feel that there was a world war anywhere. Now I am going to see a performance about America. It promises to be interesting, and it distracts me from my own thoughts.

BREMEN, 1946. AUGUST 16, FRIDAY

I got to know a young man from Yugoslavia during a dance one evening. Mio is his name. He is pleasant and has offered to arrange that we will leave on the ship on the twenty-second. He will go at the same time. We will drag the days out here together, days that seem to pass so slowly. Everybody is impatient by now, wishing to get to America as soon as possible. We all have had enough of life in the camps.

Last evening they showed a film again, this time about the Russian war. I was crying. I wept and I buried the past, the war, the suffering, and Europe—I said good-bye to everything that hurts, and from now on I only want to look forward. I had enough of the past. I wrote to my American relatives. I find it very moving that I will finally meet them, and I am curious how they will receive me.

Here in Germany I got into the habit of smoking cigarettes, and I am starting to become a true smoker. So far I wore my hair pinned up, but Mio would not leave me in peace and I have no excuse that it is more comfortable because of the heat (you cannot even speak about real heat here), so I let my hair down again the old fashioned way. Life in this camp suits me well because I do not have the possibility to gain weight, just the contrary in fact. Breakfast is only till nine o'clock, which I usually miss, lunch is not much, and neither is the dinner. Slowly I run out of the things I brought with me, and you cannot get anything in this place. Oh well, finally there are only six days, and we will be on the ship. I don't remember when I was counting the days with such difficulty or when the days seemed to be so long. To kill time we played chess, Ping-Pong, or went into the city. One evening we saw the operetta "Vetter von Dingsola"; it was quite nice in its way. Tonight we will dance again, and tomorrow is Mio's birthday. It is so difficult to celebrate it since there is nothing here to buy, not even a bottle of liqueur.

The weather is often overcast. It rains, or the sun shines, sometimes both at the same time. I still don't know what I will do once I get there; I will have to wait for whatever fate or a stroke of luck will bring me. I said good-bye to everyone, and I closed all unfinished business. I am ready for the new life, a powerful change almost like at the start of the war when I moved away from home to live under a different name, cut off from family and friends. And again it is before me to save my mother, just like then. Life has repetitions, only the surroundings are different. It will be good to have normal postal contact again. How many plans I have, my goodness! To send my mom money and packages, and as for me I would like to study further. Mio plans to study to be a reporter. Should I try to do the same?

BREMENHAFEN, 1946. AUGUST 22, THURSDAY

Departure. Everything is packed and ready; we are only waiting for them to gather the luggage and sound the bugle call. It is almost unbelievable that I live to experience such crucial hours, that only in a short time I leave Europe, and we put off to the ocean from this foggy, rainy, cold port to the warm sunshine.

And then I will set eyes on America! I wonder whether I will return here, where I spent twenty-two years, the first twenty-two years of my life, where I suffered a lot but also learned a lot, where I was brought up with good education, where I honed my ambitions, where I was shown the way toward the future. I also wonder how much of my dreams I will be able to fulfill, how much will be realized from my ambitions. And will I be able to show those whom I am leaving in this part of the world that it was worthwhile to leave here, to flee from the past and from myself to search elsewhere for happiness

Will I find my happiness there in America??

MY VOYAGE TO AMERICA

MARINE PERCH, 1946. AUGUST 23, FRIDAY

I feel like a kid on the ship, so happy with the waves surrounding us, the English-speaking stewards bustling about, and especially the new money. From now on I will be thinking only in dollars, the dollar, America's money—and now exchanging hands before my eyes my money too. Last night I got to know the *dime* and the *nickel* and what they really were when I bought my first Coke in the canteen.

It is a wonderful feeling to sail on this ship on the way toward America and to know that in a couple of days I will catch sight of New York. Somehow it is still unbelievable when I reflect on all this. I fall into various moods, from fun-loving laughter to deep anguish, while I observe the foaming waves as they move away from the stern of the ship that is taking us to another land, another country. I recall the past, a time way back before the war. Poor Otti entered my mind. How young he was when fate cut away his future, how much he could have offered to so many others with his talents, his gaiety! Or was it this tragedy that saved him from even more horrid experiences that the war would have caused him?

Today the clock was turned back one hour; we will live six hours more by traveling through all the time zones. This is also a gift from life during such pleasant conditions. Physically life is very good on the ship; the food is excellent, the air, the weather, the sunshine, all contribute to a certain physical wellbeing, the soul's total satisfaction with the present, to be able to look forward to an interesting and promising future that radiates a wonderful harmony. I am not talking now about worries and problems, which pop up now and then. What is my view of the future? I am full of mixed feelings; I have no idea what I will be doing. I only know one thing, and that is to have a carrier. How and by what means, I don't know, but I will trust my chance, my luck, and fate. I will let my destiny move along like an avalanche that rolls up my adventures and personal experiences, sealing them forever while it strengthens and swells up along the way and becomes powerful and dangerous.

MARINE PERCH, 1946. AUGUST 24, SATURDAY

Today the weather is a bit overcast. The surge of the ocean is stronger and many are lying down seasick, among them my cousin Laci. Luckily I am absolutely well, regarding the seasickness, only my throat swelled up last night. I hope as soon as the sun comes out it will go away. After breakfast, which I enjoyed as much as always, I talked to a major and other Americans. They gave me oranges, which are good for the stomach at such times. I cannot get over the beauty of the present moment, gliding on the ocean toward the next land, when so much new and unexpected is awaiting you. I already got used to the small ways of the New World on this ship, the order of the meals, the meal itself, and generally life on the ship, an American territory.

The passengers are quite boorish, often irritating. Even though the ship is fitted for the DPs, (Displaced Persons) they are only a small percentage here. One's blood can boil seeing so many Nazis around. The Americans had no idea that those who have American citizenships, just because they were born in the United States, could actually have been fighting with the Germans during the war and now are in a hurry to return to the US to vanish from any retributive consequences. They got the nicest cabins, and they sit in the big dining room while we are in the belly of the ship. But I am not complaining. However, one thing is certain: if in ten to fifteen years I return for a visit to Europe, I will not go on this kind of ship. Either it will be on a luxury liner or by plane. But for now it is real happiness to be even on this troop ship, without any comfort and luxury, but happy, perhaps much happier than sometime during a future return when perhaps a thousand disappointments will be behind me!

MARINE PERCH, 1946. AUGUST 29, THURSDAY (MIDNIGHT)

The day after tomorrow morning we will be in New York. All day today I was in an odd mood. Somehow I have the same feeling as when I said good-bye to Jozsi and I went to Munich; he on the other hand went to Bruxelles. I was afraid that I will have no one to direct me, help me, and give me advice. Still I must say that I succeeded. I seem to have been dealt the kind of life in which I have to fight for everything myself. I sent a telegram to Uncle Max, but so far I've got no answer. Perhaps that is the reason I have such an uncertain feeling in me. I imagine myself in that humongous city as a lost little worm who does not know among the multitude how to gasp for breath or which way to go in all the confusion.

Sometimes I would like to hold back, slow down this ship, for we should not travel so fast. We are living in such a nice, worry-free and timeless period that will never happen in my life again. The waves are full of hope and expectation. I am living a wonderful dream that moves ahead mercilessly and carries me closer to the unknown future full of worries and problems. I have a thousand questions in me and not one idea which would answer them. Standing on the deck, watching the waves leaving us, I have flashbacks of some crucial moments in my life when I experienced the most dangerous situations and when circumstances put me to the greatest test. Perhaps I was hoping that these memories will leave me forever together with the billows. And now I realized that I was actually a very serious actress in a real drama. The only difference was that there was no writer who wrote my lines and no director coaching and directing the play. I had to act in the most important moments, instinctively, with the utmost calm and with absolute self-assurance because if I would show any alarm, it would have cast a shadow of suspicion on my sincerity and would put my life immediately at risk.

Oh well, the important thing is that I got this far and that in only one more night, I will catch sight of the American shore.

I suffered a lot of privations. I had many close calls threatening my life. I was hungry, I was lonely, heartbroken, and forsaken by all, but lo and behold, here I am. I left all that behind me.

I MADE IT!

EPILOGUE

This is what I learned later, when I was already living in New York.

In Hungary, 600,000 Jews were murdered.

I never heard from any witness what happened to my dear father. His last days were with the other men on the truck that took him to the transit camp and from there to the death march toward Austria. None of the men from that building came back. My mother had him declared legally dead in 1949 and inscribed his name on the black granite tombstone that stands in the cemetery in Miskolc where my Drucker grandparents are buried on the Avas hill. Later, when I revisited Miskolc, my birthplace, I had a marble plaque placed on the wall of the Jewish temple on the Kazinczi street in his memory.

When I arrived in New York City in 1946, my relatives waited for me at the port. My first impression upon looking around was the funny straw hats with colorful floral ribbons that men wore. This did not exist in Europe. Uncle Max and his brother Ben picked me up and took me in a taxi to the Bronx, while my cousin Laci was picked up by his relatives in a fancy Cadillac.

From here on I did not see much of him. So much for the gratitude that I brought him with me to America. Without me he could not have made one step alone. I stayed with my relatives in their modest home; it was impossible to find an apartment. Since the soldiers came back after the war and there were no apartments built for years, they also had to move in with their parents, even after they got married.

My relatives had lived here for thirty years. Max worked as a typesetter in a printing shop, and Malvin still could only manage her English to do the shopping at the market. She did not appreciate the fact that I spoke English perfectly. Actually the great advantage I enjoyed through my trip in Europe ended the day I landed here. Everybody spoke English in America. My relatives were not well off, and though they tried to help me, the general atmosphere was not friendly toward people like me, who were called "greenhorns." They did not empathize with me going through a world war; they had no idea what it meant to live through it and survive. I was pressured to get married since all the girls around me got married right after high school at age eighteen, and by then I was twenty-two years old.

I was introduced in December to an American Jewish veteran with Hungarian roots, and by April 1947 we got married and lived for two years in Port Chester, New York. From there we moved to Greenwich, Connecticut, and opened a jewelry store. I learned the business and worked full time. My son was born in 1950. I got my citizenship in two years and thus was able to bring my mother to the United States as a legal immigrant. I was hoping that she would help me out with the baby since I had to work in the store, but she did not stay long with us and moved to New York City. With the GI Bill we bought a small house in Cos Cob, Connecticut; it made me very proud to own a piece of America.

My cousin Dudi survived Auschwitz, having contacted typhoid there and luckily saved by the liberating forces. Her husband, Frici, died of tuberculosis. She went to Prague, where she met her old friend from Kassa (now Kosice), who became a dentist at the Prague University. They got married and later emigrated to Australia.

I never heard from Julie again. I had no way to look for her, but she knew our address in Budapest and was not looking for us. I am still forever grateful to her for teaching me English, which helped me through my entire life.

My cousin Zsuzska left us in Budapest and moved to Prague, where she attended the university. When she was able to get in touch with her relatives in Argentina, they helped her emigrate to Buenos Aires from there.

At the same time my cousin Robi also went to Prague and studied to become an engineer. From there he left for Israel and took part as an officer in four wars, working as a mine detector.

Gyuri, the love of my life, was lost on the Russian front. No one knew anything about him. His loss has changed my life forever.

Six of my Jewish classmates survived: two came to the United States, and the other four remained in Budapest and are living well.

My cousin Laci, whom I helped to escape from Hungary and brought him with me to New York City, left after a short stay, married a Hungarian woman, and moved to Chicago. I never heard from him again, and to this day I don't know if he is alive or not. He was ten years older than I.

Our large family of seventy members in Kassa were all deported, and no one came back. Now I have only my immediate family near me. After six years of marriage I got a divorce, and in 1955 remarried a Hungarian Jewish immigrant; his past, upbringing, and tradition were like mine. We had two more sons, and all three are very talented, wonderful people. Unfortunately they have no aunts, uncles, or cousins and thus also feel the impact of the holocaust.

When my husband started a men's shoe import business, I gave up the jewelry store. We moved to Manhattan, and I joined him, including traveling to Italy. After a couple of years, we moved to Florence with the family and spent four beautiful years there, the best years of our lives. We returned to the United States to have our boys attend university in America and lived in Tappan, New York, a lovely old historical hamlet, until the boys left the parental home and we retired to Florida.

I am proud of the fact that I stood my ground in a new—and to me—strange country, with no support from anyone. With time I established or re-created a lifestyle to the same standard that I was brought up in before Hitler destroyed everything and murdered all my loved ones. The years of my youth that I lost, and all its consequences, can never be compensated.

Meanwhile my mother moved to Miami Beach, Florida, and she died at age ninety-one. My husband and I have settled down in Miami, where we enjoy our golden years in a condominium surrounded by a beautiful tropical garden. Two of my sons are married, and I have five grandchildren. The middle son is a happy bachelor. Sadly none of them live close by; however, I take advantage of the twenty-first century's technology, which allows me to keep in touch with all of them by e-mail and Skype; it lets me enjoy my old age together with my husband, who turned ninety years old last May. Translating my old diary became my new occupation and a fulfillment in my life.

MIAMI, FLORIDA. NOVEMBER 27, 2011

(70.)

megváltozott arcát, játszó gyerekeket, és a mozik előcsarnokában a karácsonyfát, villanygyertyákkal díszítve. Fekete karácsony van, még a csillogó havat sem élvezhetem, mely a lábam alatt ropog. Most hiányzik a Patak utca, amelyen minden reggel keresztül mentem, a táskával kezemben, Bocskay sapkával a fejemen, sötétkék kabátban, és csúnya, diákos magos barna cipőm alatt ropogott a friss, magas hó. Az arcom kipirult, és körülöttem csupa arodáru pajzos leányarc igyekezett az iskolába. Milyen régnek tűnik, milyen távolban lebeg előttem ez a kép! De még éles és tiszta, mint az a napos téli reggel. Két oldalt látom a két öreg ecetfát, jobbra a kanyargó piszkos Peret, mely ilyenkor fejéslen befagyott, és mintha hallom a kerítés mögül ugató kutyát. És hogy miért, nem tudom, de most is benézek lelki szememmel egy ablakba, ahol egy íróasztalon egy réz bagoly áll, szárnyát kifeszítve. A Gyuri egykori szobája. Milyen régen elköltözött Gyuri már onnan, de én azért minden reggel benéztem meg szokásból? Vagy azt vártam, hogy egyszercsak kikönyököl mosolyogva, mint valamikor régen? Nem tudom.

A PAGE FROM THE ORIGINAL HAND WRITTEN DIARY

Made in the USA
Lexington, KY
13 December 2016